T0072455

Cambridge Elements ≡

Elements in Publishing and Book Culture
edited by
Samantha Rayner
University College London
Leah Tether
University of Bristol

PUBLICATION AND THE PAPACY IN LATE ANTIQUITY AND THE MIDDLE AGES

Samu Niskanen

University of Helsinki

CAMBRIDGE
UNIVERSITY PRESS

CAMBRIDGE
UNIVERSITY PRESS

University Printing House, Cambridge CB2 8BS, United Kingdom

One Liberty Plaza, 20th Floor, New York, NY 10006, USA

477 Williamstown Road, Port Melbourne, VIC 3207, Australia

314–321, 3rd Floor, Plot 3, Splendor Forum, Jasola District Centre,
New Delhi – 110025, India

103 Penang Road, #05–06/07, Visioncrest Commercial, Singapore 238467

Cambridge University Press is part of the University of Cambridge.

It furthers the University's mission by disseminating knowledge in the pursuit of
education, learning, and research at the highest international levels of excellence.

www.cambridge.org
Information on this title: www.cambridge.org/9781009111089
DOI: 10.1017/9781009109864

First published 2021

A catalogue record for this publication is available from the British Library.

ISBN 978-1-009-11108-9 Paperback
ISSN 2514-8524 (online)
ISSN 2514-8516 (print)

Publication and the Papacy in Late Antiquity and the Middle Ages

Elements in Publishing and Book Culture

DOI: 10.1017/9781009109864

First published online: December 2021

Samu Niskanen

University of Helsinki

Author for correspondence: Samu Niskanen, samu.niskanen@helsinki.fi

ABSTRACT: This Element explores the papacy's engagement in authorial publishing in late antiquity and the Middle Ages. The opening discussion demonstrates that throughout the medieval period, papal involvement in the publication of new works was a phenomenon, which surged in the eleventh century. The efforts by four authors to use their papal connexions in the interests of publicity are examined as case studies. The first two are St Jerome and Arator, late-antique writers who became highly influential partly due to their declaration that their literary projects enjoyed papal sanction. Appreciation of their publication strategies sets the scene for a comparison with two eleventh-century authors, Fulcoius of Beauvais and St Anselm. This Element argues that papal involvement in publication could constitute a powerful promotional technique. It is a hermeneutic that brings insights into both the aspirations and concerns of medieval authors. This title is also available as Open Access on Cambridge Core.

KEYWORDS: papacy, patronage, medieval history, late antiquity, manuscripts

ISBNs: 9781009111089 (PB), 9781009109864 (OC)

ISSNs: 2514-8524 (online), 2514-8516 (print)

Contents

1 Introduction

Publishing is a social act involving at base two parties: an author and their intended audience. More often than not, other agents, such as patrons, commissioners, printers and booksellers, contribute to the process. The same thing applies to authorial publishing in manuscript cultures, except that scribes and other artisans replace printers among those ancillary actors. A more profound but related disparity is that publishing in manuscript, if successful, is a more prolonged affair than using the printing press. It is prone to consist of various 'publishing moments', that is, authorial interventions to expedite distribution, which may take place long after the first release.[1] To ensure dissemination in the era before print, texts most often had to be released several times. Under such circumstances, networking would have been of fundamental importance. Accordingly, it has recently been argued that 'publishing circles' embracing 'individuals and institutions which were actively engaged in the authorial effort to spread the text' were integral to authorial publication in the Middle Ages.[2] This book is an investigation of such auxiliary agency by the greatest single source of ecclesiastical power in the late-antique and medieval West, the papacy. The following case studies explore how four writers propagated their association with the pope or a party acting in an apostolic capacity in order to disseminate their writings, and what sort of results followed their attempts. It should be added that anonymous works were abundant in the age of the manuscript book, be they accidentally or deliberately separated from their authors' names, such as to be a far more present consideration in

---

[1] D. Hobbins, *Authorship and Publicity Before Print: Jean Gerson and the Transformation of Late Medieval Learning* (Philadelphia: University of Pennsylvania Press, 2009), p. 154.

[2] J. Tahkokallio, *The Anglo-Norman Historical Canon: Publishing and Manuscript Culture* (Cambridge University Press, 2019), pp. 2, 8–9. For previous conceptualisations of authorial publishing before print, see ibid., pp. 3–9 and S. Niskanen, 'The emergence of an authorial culture: publishing in Denmark in the long twelfth century', in A. C. Horn and K. G. Johansson (eds.), *The Meaning of Media. Texts and Materiality in Medieval Scandinavia* (Berlin: De Gruyter, 2021), pp. 71–91, at 71–5.

publication then than they are now. Nonetheless, in attempts to observe and explain the complexities of how authors of any period sought to obtain audiences, a natural starting point for investigation – and what might be considered the single most important external attribute for any work – is authorial identity. It is for that reason that identifiable authors were selected for scrutiny here. Even so, anonymous writings do feature in the following pages and the subject of anonymous publication will be given brief consideration in Chapter 5.1.[3]

The subject of papal engagement in authorial domains in the era of the manuscript book remains for the most part uncharted territory. The current state of research is at least in part the result of a scholarly focus on prohibitive measures such as book-burnings and official prescriptions for control over what could be published and read, culminating in the emergence of the *Index librorum prohibitorum* in the sixteenth century.[4] While those enquiries are certainly valuable, the emphasis on censorship is

---

[3] What can be classified as scribal publication, in which copyists and redactors rather than authors were the central protagonists, likewise falls outside the remit of this study; see L. Tether, 'Revisiting the manuscripts of Perceval and the continuations: Publishing practices and authorial transition', *Journal of the International Arthurian Society*, 2 (2015), 20–45; L. Tether, *Publishing the Grail in Medieval and Renaissance France* (Woodbridge: Boydell and Brewer, 2017); S. Niskanen, 'Copyists and redactors: Towards a prolegomenon to the *editio princeps* of *Peregrinatio Antiochie per Vrbanum papam facta*', in O. Merisalo, M. Kuha and S. Niiranen (eds.), *Transmission of Knowledge in the Late Middle Ages and the Renaissance* (Turnhout: Brepols, 2019), pp. 103–14. The term 'scribal publication' is admittedly problematic in that in early modern contexts it is used to distinguish between dissemination in manuscript and in print, for which see H. Love, *Scribal Publication in Seventeenth-Century England* (Oxford: Clarendon Press, 1993).

[4] For papal precensorship, see D. H. Wiest, *The Precensorship of Books (Canons 1384–1386, 1392–1394, 2318,§2). A History and a Commentary* (Washington, DC: The Catholic University of America Press, 1953); for book-burnings by papal and other agents, see T. Werner, *Den Irrtum liquidieren: Bücherverbrennungen im Mittelalter* (Göttingen: Vandenhoeck & Ruprecht, 2007).

one-sided. The approach yields a narrative in which the active role is reserved for Rome, reducing writers to victims at the receiving end of whatever proscription had been enacted. That narrative is distorted. For, at least in the late-antique and medieval periods, the positive prospects for publication that could flow from the involvement of Rome must have outweighed the restrictive ones.

That suggestion derives from a quantitative survey undertaken as part of the project *Medieval Publishing* at the University of Helsinki. The corpus of the survey embraced all medieval prefatory texts found in the 217 volumes of the *Patrologia Latina* (henceforth *PL*), which brings together Christian Latin writings from the late second century to the early thirteenth. The texts in question number in the thousands. They were searched in order to identify all literary works in whose publication a papal party – the pope and members of his administrative apparatus – partook as authors, commissioners or dedicatees or occupied other pertinent roles.[5] Before turning to discuss the results relevant to this study, I must first introduce the chief caveats. Letters not classifiable as treatises, short individual poems or texts produced in the course of business (such as administrative and legal documents, minutes of assemblies and so on) were excluded in the survey.[6] While these are often loose categories, individual texts had to be classified without meticulous deliberation, on account of the vast extent of the corpus. The *PL* is far from a comprehensive omnibus and a flawless source. It offers a selection moulded by what was available and of interest to Jacques-Paul Migne (†1875), the general editor of the series. His misattributions and errors were legion.[7] Better editions

---

[5] I thank Lauri Marjamäki for carrying out this laborious enterprise.

[6] For poems addressed to the pope, see T. Haye, *Päpste und Poeten. Die mittelalterliche Kurie als Objekt und Förderer panegyrischer Dichtung* (Berlin: De Gruyter, 2009).

[7] R. H. Bloch, *God's Plagiarist: Being an Account of the Fabulous Industry and Irregular Commerce of the Abbé Migne* (Chicago University Press, 1994).

and secondary works were naturally consulted as part of our survey, but universal verification would have required years of work. Nonetheless, irrespective of the *PL*'s serious imperfections, what its enormous corpus yields on a large scale provides the foundation for further inquiries into Christian Latin literature. The important consideration here is that it is vanishingly unlikely that the *PL* could have committed systematic error in its inclusion of pieces from the period whose publication involved a party acting in an apostolic capacity. Out of the 217 volumes, forty-nine convey such texts. The quantity bespeaks a real phenomenon. Figure 1 summarises the rate of recurrence as a ratio of the said group of forty-nine volumes to all volumes. The horizontal bar complies, by and large, with chronological span from the late second century to the early thirteenth.

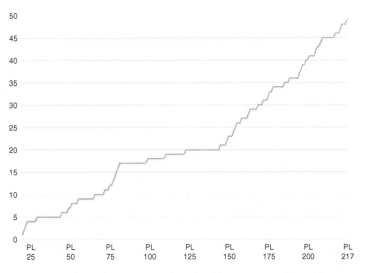

Figure 1 Papal involvement in authorial publication as evidenced by *PL*

The first upsurge, at *PL* 75–9, is contingent on the contribution of one man and his networks, Pope Gregory the Great (†604). As such the curve is not demonstrative of a trend. The second escalation, beginning at *PL* 144–5, carrying Peter Damian's (†1072) oeuvre, suggests a steady increase from the mid-eleventh century to the end of the period surveyed. That expansion seems to correlate with the intensification of papal activism from the 1050s onwards, a trend termed as reform papacy (or similar) in modern scholarship. Adherents of that papal movement were increasingly driven to reinforce the papacy's position at the head of ecclesiastical hierarchies in order to ensure that the standards of the church and the lives of the faithful across Latin Christendom could be improved under apostolic guidance. To intervene in local affairs, popes had to assume new powers, expand the apparatus of their government and extend their reach to regions remote from Rome by creating proxies. Our survey hints that the mounting extent of papal intervention in authorial domains was connected to those policies. If so, the situation created new opportunities for writers.

Equipped with that preliminary quantitative perception, this book explores in qualitative terms how writers could benefit from Rome. Four writers have been selected for scrutiny: Jerome (†420), Arator (†544 or after), Fulcoius of Beauvais (apparently †1119 or after) and Anselm of Bec and Canterbury (†1109).[8] The rationale behind the selection is as follows. First, Jerome and Arator, major Latin authors, provide two very significant cases of conspicuous papal engagement in publication from the first centuries. Jerome's Latin translation of the Gospels, undertaken in the 380s, became one of the most read books in the West and remained so until the emergence of vernacular translations in the late Middle Ages. His emphasis that he worked under papal commission was cherished in subsequent reception to the degree of serious overstatement. Arator, a sixth-century epicist of the Bible, was read for centuries by students of Latin verse. The first issue of his work, *Historia apostolica*, was

---

[8] I am only aware of one previous commentary on multiple authors from a viewpoint comparable to that of this study: A. Paravicini Bagliani, 'Le dediche alla corte dei papi nel duecento e l'autocoscienza intellettuale', *Filologia mediolatina*, 17 (2010), 69–84.

a splendid event staged by the pope, a short description of which is found in dozens of manuscripts. Secondly, Jerome and Arator, in that their recourse to papal sanction in their publishing was so obvious, provide us with hermeneutics to read publishing by other authors in fresh ways, even if direct influences cannot be shown. This applies to Anselm and Fulcoius. Anselm's authorial alliance with the papacy parallels Jerome's in that criticisms against their methodological approaches – radical departures at the time – were significant factors in both cases. Arator's publishing career furnishes a framework by which the authorial ambitions and eventual failure of Fulcoius of Beauvais can be appreciated more precisely than before. In the company of three extremely successful writers, Fulcoius also offers a healthy antidote to the potential misconception that an appeal to the pope would necessarily have secured wide readerships. Thirdly, our quantitative survey suggests that the reform papacy's activist programme as it took shape in the latter half of the eleventh century may have multiplied Rome's active collaborations with authors. Anselm and Fulcoius offer us contrasting insights into papal policies towards authorial publication in that crucial period. Rich in implication, evidence on Anselm also presents starting points for further considerations of how the papacy's affirmative interventions in publication resonated with its claims to the prerogative over censorship.

2 Jerome and Pope Damasus

One of the most significant publication projects in which the papacy has ever engaged must be the Latin translation of the Gospels by Jerome of Stridon (†420) under commission from Pope Damasus (†384).[9] The objective was to address the problem that several older Latin translations were being transmitted, of variable quality. These are now referred to under the collective title *Vetus Latina*. Jerome, an excellent linguist who had worked in papal administration, was assigned to amend the Latin text by recourse to the authentic Greek. Undertaken in the course of nearly three years in Rome, from 382 to 385, the new translation proved a success. After the first publication and Pope Damasus' death, Jerome and others made new Latin translations of all the books of the Bible, including the Hebrew Old Testament. The outcome is what is now called the Vulgate, a title which derives from the medieval nickname *Versio vulgata*, 'a version for the people', that is, a version in common use. The Vulgate eventually replaced the *Vetus Latina* translations, a process that was only completed centuries later. In what follows, Jerome's translations of parts of the Bible other than the Gospels are not attended to, as our focus is exclusively on those of his writings in whose publication the papacy was involved in one way or another. These will be studied through the prism of his career.

Born in Stridon in Dalmatia in 347 or 348, Jerome had a peripatetic career. It took him to Rome, Trier, Aquileia, Antioch, Syria, Constantinople, back to Rome and then back to the East where he died, in Bethlehem. Like other learned men with complex trajectories, Jerome was seeking work and patronage. The papal court was his target in the 370s, as may be inferred from two letters he addressed to Pope Damasus from the Syrian desert near Chalcis in 376 or so. Jerome did not have any previous connexion to Damasus, and his letters read as something like

---

[9] For a more comprehensive account on Jerome's relationship with Damasus, see A. Cain, *The Letters of Jerome: Asceticism, Biblical Exegesis, and the Construction of Christian Authority in Late Antiquity* (Oxford University Press, 2009), pp. 43–67 and J. N. D. Kelly, *Jerome. His Life, Writings, and Controversies* (New York: Harper & Row, 1975), pp. 80–90.

calling cards.[10] The first sought to consult the pope on trinitarian heresies running rampant in the East and on a schism between three claimants to the see of Antioch. Jerome drew a contrast between epidemic discord and heterodoxy in the East with the West's steadfast compliance with Catholic orthodoxy under the pope's guidance. The letter also explicated the debated issue of the terms *hypostasis* and *ousia*, used to expound the concept of the Trinity. The longest of the letter's discussions, it was a deft display of Jerome's theological expertise. To ensure that Damasus' response would reach him, Jerome advised that it be carried to Evagrius of Antioch, one of the staunchest papal advocates in the East. This neatly certified Jerome's association with local supporters of Rome.[11] As an answer was not forthcoming, Jerome wrote again to the pope. This letter was a short restatement of the essence of his previous inquiry. A willingness to relocate from Syria was now implied in clearer terms with the stress that in the schism at Antioch Jerome's loyalty was to Rome alone.[12] Two letters in concert assigned such prerogatives to Rome as echoed Damasus' perceptions of papal primacy; be it a theological issue or a disputed election, the pope prevailed over other patriarchs. A later communiqué, to be discussed below in Chapter 2.2, implies that this second letter also failed to elicit a response.[13]

Within a year or two of his futile attempt to form a connexion with the papacy, Jerome left Syria for Constantinople. He was taught there by Bishop Gregory Nazianzen, one of the foremost theologians of the age.[14] Gregory was a major source of power in Constantinople and beyond, but

---

[10] Jerome, *Epp.* 15 and 16 ed. I. Hilberg, *CSEL*, 54–6 (1910–1918). For these two letters, see Cain, *Letters of Jerome*, pp. 32–3 with references to previous scholarship.

[11] A. Cain, 'The letter collections of Jerome of Stridon', in C. Sogno, B. K. Storin and E. J. Watts (eds.), *Late Antique Letter Collections: A Critical Introduction and Reference Guide* (Oakland: University of California Press, 2017), pp. 221–38, at 237 n. 89.

[12] Jerome, *Ep.* 16.2.   [13] Ibid., 35.1.

[14] Ibid., 50.1, 52.8 and *De uiris illustribus*, 117, ed. E. Richardson, *Texte und Untersuchungen zur Geschichte der altchristlichen Literatur*, 14, 1a (Leipzig: Hinrichs, 1896), pp. 1–56.

affiliation to his circle apparently could not provide for a man whose main interest was translation from Greek to Latin. Furthermore, after Gregory's resignation from office and withdrawal to Cappadocia in 381, Jerome could no longer benefit by his direct patronage.[15] The papal court remained Jerome's target. Opportunity knocked in 382 as the bishops of Antioch and Salamis attended a council at Rome and needed a Latin translator. The job was given to Jerome, and in the course of the council, his skills were recognised. Pope Damasus, who presided, assigned him to the drafting of a recantation for Bishop Apollinaris of Laodicea to denounce his Christological teachings as heresy.[16] Jerome was inducted into the papal circle.

Jerome's Roman sojourn only lasted 'nearly three years', from 382 to 385, but he acted swiftly and with determination.[17] At Constantinople, he had written two short commentaries on Isaiah 6.[18] At Rome, he submitted the pieces to Damasus. This is suggested by his incorporating them in his letter collection, each furnished with the heading 'Ad Damasum' ('To Damasum'). He also presented the pope with a Latin translation of two homilies of Origen († *c*.253) on the *Song of Songs*. Its short dedicatory proem opens with praise for Origen's immense commentary on the *Song of Songs*. In Jerome's view, that work was an unmatched tour de force, of which the two translated homilies only offered 'a foretaste'. He had to 'pass over that work because its translation would require a great deal of time, effort and funding'.[19] Jerome was soliciting for some papal commission, a plan that might be said to have miscarried.

---

[15] For Gregory's prestige in Constantinople from 379 to 381 and its subsequent decline, see B. K. Storin, *Self-Portrait in Three Colors: Gregory of Nazianzus's Epistolary Autobiography* (Oakland: University of California Press, 2019), p. 152.

[16] Rufinus, *De adulteratione librorum Origenis*, xiii, ed. M. Simonetti, *CCSL*, 20 (1961), p. 15.

[17] Jerome, *Ep.* 45.2: 'paene certe triennio'.

[18] Ibid., 18A+B. For the place of composition, see Jerome, *Commentariorum in Esaiam libri I–XI*, ed. M. Adriaen, *CCSL*, 73 (1963), p. 84.

[19] Jerome, *Praefatio in Origenis homiliis II in Canticum*, ed. W. A. Baehrens, *Corpus Berolinense*, 33 (Berlin: Brandenburgische Akademie der Wissenschaften, 1925), p. 26: '. . . illo opere praetermisso, quia ingentis est otii, laboris et sumptuum,

2.1 A New Latin Translation of the Gospels

He managed to secure a far grander commission, a revision of the Latin text of the Gospels. It is hard to think of a publication project that would have rivalled the ambition and implication of an attempt to take control of the form in which the Gospels were circulated. A new definitive text would replace the variety of earlier translations 'dispersed around the whole world', on Jerome's word.[20] There were various obstacles to achieving that goal. Jerome and Damasus must have understood that even in the most optimistic scenario its accomplishment would take a very long time. The production of manuscript copies was time-consuming; the pope did not possess a prerogative and powers to impose a new translation on local churches; operations to spread copies swiftly over long distances had to be created on an ad hoc basis (something that was indeed done, as will be shown in due course). What is more, *Vetus Latina* translations had shaped the vocabulary and communication of the Christian experience for generations. Telling testimonies of the impact of the *Vetus Latina* exist in phrases and formulations that were rejected from the Vulgate but remain in Christian use even today.[21] To overcome that challenge, Jerome prefixed a proem to his translation. This took the form of a dedicatory letter, an antique literary device by which authors could simultaneously address their patrons and intended readerships. Jerome's dedicatee was his commissioner, Pope Damasus, who is saluted in the letter's address clause and conclusion. The argument in the proem, however, was directed to wider readerships.

In its first half, the proem seeks explicitly to justify the project by explaining its rationale. The translation had been prompted by the fact that available Latin translations frequently disagreed with each other and

---

tantas res, tamque dignum opus in Latinum transferre sermonem, hos duos tractatus . . . fideliter magis quam ornate interpretatus sum: gustum tibi sensuum eius, non cibum offerens . . .'.

[20] Jerome, *Praefatio in Euangelio*, *Biblia Sacra iuxta Vulgatam Versionem*, ed. R. Weber, 3rd ed. (Stuttgart: Deutsche Bibelgesellschaft, 1983), p. 1515: 'toto orbe dispersa'.

[21] For instance, the papal encyclical *Lumen Fidei* of 2013 quotes the *Vetus Latina* rendition of Isaiah 7:9 'si non credideritis, non intellegetis'.

rendered the Greek original imperfectly. A plethora of inaccuracies had been introduced already in the process of translation and many more had emerged in the course of manuscript transmission, which subjected texts to scribal slips and deliberate interventions. Referring to those central vagaries of copying by hand, Jerome articulated a case for reverting to the Greek original. He emphasised that the New Testament and the Old Testament were two quite different entities in respect of translation. The latter was available in two authoritative forms, the Hebrew original and the Septuagint, a Greek translation. The commanding status of the Septuagint flowed from endorsement by the writers of the New Testament, whose citations from the Old Testament were often recognisably of that translation. The case of the New Testament was more straightforward in that there was a single fountainhead, the original Greek text. Devoid of endorsement by biblical authors, Latin translations were derivatives of inferior status. In their divergence from the Greek original they could make no claim to divinely inspired authenticity. To put it more bluntly, Latin deviations were errors.

This was a daring proposition at the time. Because formal and private devotion had built on *Vetus Latina* articulations for generations, these enjoyed the status of a received text. That aspect was relevant to the Gospels in particular. They took precedence over all other books of the Christian Bible and their reception history reflects this. In the corpus of extant Latin manuscripts dating roughly from before the ninth century, the Bible more often than not was transmitted in partial copies rather than as volumes embracing all its books. Copies of the Gospels predominate throughout these early centuries. The high proportion of gospelbooks among the survivors may belong to one or both of two factors: that the Gospels were copied more often; and that copies were of higher quality as books, therefore more valued as possessions and therefore enjoying more favourable conditions for survival.[22] Either way, it is clear that the Gospels were the most treasured of biblical books. Jerome was acutely aware that he

---

[22] P. McGurk, 'The oldest manuscripts of the Latin Bible', in R. Gameson (ed.), *The Early Medieval Bible: Its Production, Decoration and Use* (Cambridge University Press, 1994), pp. 1–23, at 2–4.

was handling a cherished, indeed venerated, text, such that even the slightest emendation could give offence. The proem to his translation offered the assurance that previous readings had been preserved intact wherever possible, which they were for the most part, and that only errors distorting the sense had been corrected.[23] It is true that his interventions were rather light. They also became fewer as his work progressed.[24]

2.2 Protection by Papal Commission

The commission obtained from the pope granted Jerome requisites for his work, and it also bestowed prestige beneficial to publication. The latter is the context in which his dedicatory letter, the proem to the translation, foregrounds the address to Pope Damasus. The fact that the pope had commissioned the work is made known in the very opening sentence, as follows.

> You urge that I make a new work from an old one, that
> I should sit as something of a judge over copies of Scripture
> dispersed throughout the whole world, and that, because
> they differ from each other, I might resolve which agree
> with the Greek verity.[25]

Jerome's assertion is that his methodological preference for Greek original over Latin tradition was a papal contract which it would be a derogation to refuse. A few lines below, the commission from Damasus is referred to again. It is now presented more explicitly as a protective shield. In the midst of any criticism that might follow publication, it would be Jerome's consolation 'that you, who are the highest priest, command

---

[23] Jerome, *Praefatio in Euangelio*, ed. Weber, pp. 1515–16.

[24] H. A. G. Houghton, *The Latin New Testament: A Guide to Early History, Texts and Manuscripts* (Oxford University Press, 2016), pp. 33–4.

[25] Jerome, *Praefatio in Euangelio*, ed. Weber, p. 1515: 'Nouum opus facere me cogis ex ueteri, ut post exemplaria Scripturarum toto orbe dispersa, quasi quidam arbiter sedeam: et quia inter se uariant, quae sint illa que cum graeca ueritate decernam.'

[this translation] to be made'.[26] The party responsible for the whole affair was its commissioner, the pope.

Fears of criticism were well founded. In 384 or so, at about the time of the project's completion, Jerome informed a correspondent of his censure by 'two-legged asses' that his translation was 'against the authority of the old and the opinion of the whole world'.[27] Three epistolary exchanges between Damasus and Jerome in the course of the project imply that such criticisms had been aroused well before. In modern editions, the letters in question are *Epp.* 19 and 20, *Ep.* 21 (Jerome's response to Damasus' letter, which is incorporated in part), and *Epp.* 35 and 36. In each exchange, Damasus posed queries which had emerged from his reading of the Latin Bible, and Jerome expounded from his knowledge of Greek and Hebrew. The subtext was Jerome's hermeneutical method, its preference for authentic text in Greek and Hebrew over derivative Latin translations and commentaries.[28] Their final exchange, which is likely to have taken place in 384, is of primary interest here. In *Ep.* 35, Damasus posed five questions about biblical readings; in *Ep.* 36, Jerome responded to three and referred the pope to select commentaries as regards the remaining two.[29] Each of Damasus' questions resonated with a contemporary work, *Quaestiones Veteris et Noui Testamenti*, such that the coincidence cannot have been by chance.[30] That treatise was written by an anonymous author, who is now called Ambrosiaster, in Rome at the turn of the 370s.

What makes the resonance between Damasus' letter and *Quaestiones* more remarkable is the fact that Ambrosiaster was one of the 'two-legged asses', to quote Jerome's disdainful phrase, who disapproved of his method

---

[26] Ibid.: 'aduersum quam inuidiam duplex causa me consolatur: quod et tu qui summus sacerdos es fieri iubes, et uerum non esse quod uariat etiam maledicorum testimonio conprobatur'.

[27] Jerome, *Ep.* 27.3: 'bipedes asellos'.

[28] My reading of these letters owes much to Cain, *Letters of Jerome*, pp. 51–67, although my proposition as to the genesis of *Ep.* 35 differs from his.

[29] Jerome, *Epp.* 35 and 36 respectively.

[30] S. Lunn-Rockcliffe, *Ambrosiaster's Political Theology* (Oxford University Press, 2007), pp. 24–5; Cain, *Letters of Jerome*, pp. 59–60.

of translation. Emphasising the significance of Latin tradition, Ambrosiaster rejected the proposal that the Greek New Testament had authority over the *Vetus Latina*.[31] It is a moot point whether Jerome knew Ambrosiaster's criticism only as an anonymous report or attached to the man.[32] In either case, when read in the context of Ambrosiaster's hostility, *Epp.* 35 and 36 emerge as a defence against a specific enemy. The letters vindicated Jerome's approach by way of implication rather than explicitly. A head-on assault could have been unfeasible due to Rome's internal politics.[33] Furthermore, Jerome's later reputation as a towering biblical exegete had not yet formed other than within his own circles and those close to the pope. Damasus was an old man, and Jerome would soon have to find a new patron. Well-connected critics such as Ambrosiaster, who was apparently a presbyter at a suburban Roman church and as such enjoyed a status nearly equal to that of bishops, had to be handled with care.[34]

The question of intended audience is crucial to any attempt to construe a text in its own terms. Antique and medieval epistles were usually of a semi-public nature rather than being confidential exchanges. That public aspect was evident in the practices of their presentation to the recipient and their subsequent transmission. Letters were often recited by the courier to the addressee and others present on the occasion; copies were circulated to parties other than the addressee; several authors released their correspondence as collections.[35] Jerome was such a one

---

[31] For Ambrosiaster's apparent reaction to Jerome's denunciation, see T. S. de Bruyn, S. A. Cooper and D. G. Hunter, *Ambrosiaster's Commentary on the Pauline Epistles: Romans* (Atlanta: SBL Press, 2017), pp. xxvi–xxvii, 103 and 224–5.

[32] Kelly, *Jerome*, p. 149; A. Cain, 'In Ambrosiaster's shadow: a critical re-evaluation of the last surviving letter exchange between Pope Damasus and Jerome', *Revue d'études augustiniennes et patristiques*, 51 (2005), 257–77, at 271–2; Cain, *Letters of Jerome*, pp. 51–2; Houghton, *Latin New Testament*, pp. 25–6; Lunn-Rockcliffe, *Ambrosiaster's Political Theology*, pp. 22–3.

[33] Cain, 'Ambrosiaster's shadow', 273–4.

[34] Ibid., pp. 270–71; de Bruyn, *Ambrosiaster's Commentary on the Pauline Epistles*, pp. xxvii–xxix.

[35] For a pertinent account by Jerome, see Augustine, *Ep.* 72.1, ed. A. Goldbacher, *CSEL*, 34/2 (1898). For the varied nature of late-antique letter collections, see

to publicise his letters. As recorded in an autobiographical note at the conclusion of his *De uiris illustribus*, written in 393, the body of his writings included two discrete letter collections, *Epistolarum ad diuersos liber* and *Ad Marcellam epistolarum liber*.[36] What is more relevant to our inquiry, *De uiris illustribus* itemises his responses to Damasus' three letters individually, each under a title suggestive of a treatise, *De osanna, De frugi et luxurioso filiis* and *De tribus quaestiunculis legis ueteris*.[37] In other words, Jerome had published each of his responses as a separate piece. Furthermore, the first and third exchanges, *Epp*. 19 and 20 and *Epp*. 35 and 36 respectively, were circulated as such in the Middle Ages, hinting that he had released them as pairings, so that in both cases the papal letter preceded his response.[38]

The literary style of Damasus' queries is of relevance as to their authorial status and intention. His first two letters were business-like, conspicuously spare in their diction. The third letter, *Ep*. 35, which poses questions previously raised by Ambrosiaster, opens with an elegant allocution. Erudite allusions and refined remarks abound. The contrast to the previous two letters is such that it has been proposed that *Ep*. 35 is a forgery, which Jerome penned years after Damasus' death.[39] Today's accepted view is that the letter is genuine.[40] I would put forward a new solution, which sits between those two propositions, namely that Jerome authored the letter in part or completely, but he did so when Damasus was still alive. This scheme entails no suggestion that the letter should be taken as a forgery. For Jerome's job as a papal secretary involved letter-writing. By his testimony,

C. Sogno, B. K. Storin and E. J. Watts (eds.), *Late Antique Letter Collections: A Critical Introduction and Reference Guide* (Oakland: University of California Press, 2017).

[36] For these two collections, see Cain, 'The Letter Collections of Jerome of Stridon', 222–32 and *Letters of Jerome*, 68–98 respectively.

[37] Jerome, *De uiris illustribus*, 135. [38] Cain, *Letters of Jerome*, p. 63.

[39] P. Nautin, 'Le premier échange épistolaire entre Jérôme et Damase: lettres réelles ou fictives?', *Freiburger Zeitschrift für Philosophie und Theologie*, 30 (1983), 331–44.

[40] Cain, 'Ambrosiaster's Shadow', and *Letters of Jerome*, pp. 56–8.

Damasus had 'assigned [him] to compose ecclesiastical letters'.[41] Years after his master's death, he boasted that 'the mouth of Damasus of blessed memory [spoke] my words'.[42] Outlining *Ep.* 35 for the pope would have been within his secretarial obligations and a papal nod would have authenticated the text.

Why propose a role for Jerome in the composition of *Ep.* 35? A man of letters, Damasus was competent to compose stylish Latin prose. Several of his poems survive as inscriptions.[43] It is a debated question as to whether or not Damasus authored the *Carmen contra paganos*, an invective apparently against a certain Vettius Agorius Praetextatus. If the identification of the object of the poem's abuse is accurate, the writing took place in 384. The most recent detailed consideration, by an editor of Damasus' epigraphic poetry, concludes that the question of authorship is unanswerable; and that the candidacy of Jerome, whose disdain for Praetextatus is manifest in two roughly contemporary letters, cannot be ruled out.[44] It has also been speculated that if Damasus authored the invective, Jerome 'surely had a hand in it' and discussed the project with the pope who, at almost eighty, 'relied heavily on his new secretary'.[45] Whether such considerations pertain to *Carmen contra paganos* cannot be known for sure. Yet, they do apply to *Ep.* 35. The letter cannot have been written more than a few weeks or months before Damasus' death in 384. The man was past his prime.

The previous argument that Jerome had forged *Ep.* 35 in 387 was premised on seven verbal and phrasal analogies between it and his writings, and on certain articulations in *Ep.* 36 allegedly too impolite to represent

---

[41] Jerome, *Apologia aduersus libros Rufini*, ii.20, ed. P. Lardet, *CCSL*, 79 (1982), pp. 1–72, at 56: '. . . sub nomine cuiusdam amici Damasi, romanae urbis episcopi, ego petar, cui ille ecclesiasticas epistulas dictandas credidit . . .'. See also Jerome, *Ep.* 123.9.

[42] Jerome, *Ep.* 45.3: '[B]eatae memoriae Damasi os meus sermo erat.'

[43] For editions of the Damasian writings, see U. Reutter, *Damasus, Bischof von Rom (366–384)* (Tübingen: Mohr Siebeck, 2009) and D. Trout, *Damasus of Rome: The Epigraphic Poetry* (Oxford University Press, 2015).

[44] Ibid., pp. 30, 38.

[45] A. Cameron, *The Last Pagans of Rome* (Oxford University Press, 2011), p. 316.

genuine dialogue.[46] Much of that evidence was misread, as has been pointed out elsewhere: there is nothing rude to *Ep.* 36, while at least two of the verbal reminiscences observed between *Ep.* 35 and works by Jerome were by no means unusual phraseology at the time. Furthermore, the phrase 'furtiuis noctium operis' ('at stolen [hours] of night work'), which resonates with Jerome's *Epp.* 34.6, 114.1 and 119.1, reads as reported speech in *Ep.* 35. It was, then, a quotation from his previous communication with the pope, now lost. On the basis of these observations, the remaining Hieronymian locutions of the letter were rejected as evidence of his authorship; for they 'can be explained by this same logic of complimentary *imitatio*'.[47] The corollary would be that Damasus was very well acquainted with Jerome's other writings, especially his letters. To demonstrate whether that could be the case, we may reflect on one of the remaining cases of analogy.

> *Ep.* 35.1: I consider nothing in this world happier than such a life; all honey is surpassed by such food for the soul.[48]

> *Ep.* 30.13: [Do you know] anything happier than this plea-sure? What food, what honey is sweeter than to know God's providence?[49]

The sequence of *iucundius* ('happier') followed in the next clause by *mella* ('honey' in the plural), which cannot compare with the contemplation of God's mysteries, seems to have been a Hieronymian invention. The phrase does not appear within reported speech in *Ep.* 35. The imitation of Jerome's epistolary voice on this occasion would, then, have required familiarity with his *Ep.* 30, which also employs the phrase. Had Damasus read that letter, addressed to Marcella in 384 or so, or some other of Jerome's writings of which we are now unaware? That could hardly have

---

[46] Nautin, 'Le premier échange', 335, 337–8.

[47] Cain, 'Ambrosiaster's shadow', 261–2.

[48] 'Qua uita nihil in hac luce puto iucundius, quo animae pabulo omnia mella superantur.'

[49] 'Quid hac uoluptate iucundius? Qui cibi, quae mella sunt dulciora dei scire prudentiam?'

been the case. *Ep*. 35 betrays a lack of previous engagement with the body of Jerome's epistolary writings. This applies even to the above-discussed two letters Jerome had sent to Damasus from the Syrian desert in 376 or so. It transpires from a remark in *Ep*. 35 that the pope had failed to read and archive those two letters at the time of their dispatch in the 370s and finally did so only slightly before the writing of *Ep*. 35:

> For, because yesterday you told me via my courier that you do not have other letters [to us] except for those you once dictated in the desert, which I eagerly read and copied.[50]

A request for copies of Jerome's previous letters to him suggests that Damasus did not possess a collection of his secretary's correspondence. The situation speaks of cursory acquaintance of, rather than a scrupulous familiarity with, Jerome's epistolary writings. It should be added that Damasus' acknowledgement of Jerome's first two letters to him was long overdue. Conveyed by *Ep*. 35, the acknowledgement was received at the very last moment: months, weeks or days before Damasus' death. Such opportune timing hints at Jerome's agency. In conclusion, his three epistolary dialogues with Damasus represent a collaborative effort to affirm that his exegetical skills were more than a match for those of his critics. By no means confidential or private, the three exchanges were penned with a larger public in mind. The campaign culminated in *Epp*. 35 and 36. Jerome had by then emerged as the dominant partner, the proof of which are his fingerprints over the pope's enquiry. In his capacity as papal secretary, he had assumed the role of solicitor too. The mouth was Damasus' but the words were Jerome's.[51]

In *Ep*. 36, his last letter to Damasus, Jerome made use of his affiliation for the benefit of still another Latin translation. He observed that he 'wishes to dedicate' to the pope a translation of a treatise on the Holy Spirit, then in

---

[50] Jerome, *Ep*. 35.1: 'Itaque, quoniam et heri tabellario ad me remisso nullas te iam epistulas habere dixisti exceptis his, quas in heremo aliquando dictaueras quasque tota auiditate legi atque descripsi.'

[51] Ibid., 45.3. See n. 42 above.

progress, by Didymus, a pupil of Origen.[52] That translation was completed in Palestine three years after Damasus' death. Jerome's prologue points up the papal connexion twice, first in stating his own desire to have had the translation dedicated to Damasus, then in Damasus' injunction that he assume the project.[53] Assertions of proactive endorsement by the pope could generate an aura of authority, and the impression is that Jerome had upgraded his Didymus translation to the status of a (posthumous) papal commission. Furthermore, in a letter from the early 390s he referred to his translation of the two homilies by Origen mentioned above as having been made 'at the request of blessed Damasus at Rome'.[54] He had dedicated the translation to the pope, whereas nothing indicates that the undertaking would have been a papal request. This claim to commission by Damasus had unintended consequences.[55] Towards the end of the 390s, it was cited by Rufinus in a prologue to his translation of Origen's *On the First Principles*.[56] Origen had by then been turned into an object of fierce denunciation. Rufinus' reference to his earlier endorsement by Damasus and Jerome was a precautionary measure against criticism of Origen and the stricture that he must not be read. However, Rufinus' depiction of Jerome as Origen's enthusiastic supporter raised eyebrows in Rome, resulting in bitter strife between the two former friends.[57]

2.3 The Impact

Neither affiliation to Damasus nor a new translation of the Gospels made Jerome an established figure in Rome. He remained a client, dependent on patronage. He was criticised for too zealous promotion of monastic and ascetic ideals, and there circulated rumours of his having an affair with Paula, an aristocratic supporter.[58] Having lost papal sponsorship with

---

[52] Ibid., 36.1: 'cupio dedicare'.

[53] Jerome, *Praefatio ad Paulinianum in libro Didymi Alexandrini de Spiritu sancto*, *PL*, 23, cols. 101–3.

[54] Jerome, *Ep*. 27*.2, ed. J. Divjak, *CSEL*, 88 (1981): 'quas ammonitu beati Damasi Romae transtuli'.

[55] Cain, *Letters of Jerome*, p. 50 n. 33. [56] Jerome, *Ep*. 80.1. [57] Ibid., 83 and 84.

[58] Ibid., 45.2–3; Cain, *Letters of Jerome*, pp. 102–14.

Damasus' death in 384, a case against him was brought in an ecclesiastical court, over which Pope Siricius (†399) appears to have presided. The exact details of the indictment are unknown, but Jerome was found guilty. He left Rome humiliated in 385 and never came back.[59] Those who aligned themselves with Ambrosiaster's traditionalism in biblical exegesis were certainly pleased. Jerome's status in Rome remained precarious throughout Pope Siricius' incumbency. Subsequently, irrespective of efforts by Jerome's Roman friends, the pope chose to side with Rufinus in their widely publicised contention.[60] Jerome's absence from Rome and declining reputation there must have weakened his Gospel translation's first impact within the city. Papal recourse to the Vulgate is apparent only from Pope Zosimus onwards, incumbent in 417–18.[61]

Be that as it may, the translation found some very important contemporary readers elsewhere. The most notable among them was Augustine, bishop of Hippo in north Africa (†430). He had adopted Jerome's translation by the first years of the 400s. His *De consensu euangelistarum*, composed then, relies on Jerome's text almost throughout.[62] In a letter to Jerome, Augustine noted that the translation, which his collations with Greek manuscripts had proved to be 'virtually faultless', amounted to a considerable contribution to biblical scholarship.[63] Jerome's primary readerships also included more notorious parties. The earliest identifiable reader of Vulgate translations of New Testament books other than the Gospels, for which anonymous translators who followed Jerome's lead were responsible, was Pelagius (†418). His teachings formed the basis of Pelagianism, a set of beliefs censured as heterodox by Augustine and other contemporaries. One of the most prolific Pelagians, Julian, bishop of Eclanum († c.455), cited the Gospels from Jerome's translation.[64]

---

[59] Ibid., pp. 114–24.

[60] Jerome, *Ep.* 127.9; Jerome, *Apologia*, iii (or *Epistula aduersus Rufinum*) 21 and 24, ed. Lardet, pp. 92, 96.

[61] Houghton, *Latin New Testament*, p. 50.   [62] Ibid., pp. 36–7.

[63] Augustine, *Ep.* 71.6: 'paene in omnibus nulla offensio est cum scripturam graecam contulerimus'.

[64] Houghton, *Latin New Testament*, pp. 39–40.

No extant copy of Jerome's translation can be associated with him or his circle. But the earliest extant manuscript, most of whose leaves survive in St Gallen, Stiftsbibliothek, MS 1395 (*CLA* VII.984), is not far removed from the sphere of his influence. The book, about a half of whose extent survives in seven volumes, was made in northern Italy, possibly Verona, in the first half of the fifth century.[65] It has been speculated that some of the notes found in its margins might derive from Jerome's insertions, a proposition beyond verification.[66] In palaeographical terms, the manuscript is of mediocre quality, which, together with the absence of liturgical notes, betrays the fact that the volume was one for personal use rather than a public purpose.[67]

Institutional uses followed private. The earliest surviving Latin lectionary, the Wolfenbüttel Palimpsest, more precisely, Wolfenbüttel, Herzog-August-Bibliothek, MS Weißenburg 76 (*CLA* IX.1392), may be instanced here. The volume carries *passus* both from the Old and New Testaments to be recited in the liturgy. Those from the New Testament were taken from the Vulgate in the main, while *Vetus Latina* sources were also deployed. Dating from the first half of the sixth century, the book comes from Gaul.[68] Its liturgical application of Jerome's text is witness to penetration into communal milieux. The Wolfenbüttel Palimpsest embodies adaptation in an institution far from Rome. The book implies previous transmission in Gaul with activist engagement.

While Jerome's revision of the Gospels must have met with considerably more contemporary success than the historical record reveals, these instances were exceptions rather than the rule. The majority of Latin Gospel manuscripts preserved from the fifth to eighth centuries convey *Vetus Latina* texts. A point of interest is that various readerships did not consider Jerome's text and older translations mutually exclusive entities. A common feature of transmission was that manuscripts adopted readings both from the *Vetus Latina* and the Vulgate.[69] A case in point is the aforementioned Wolfenbüttel Palimpsest, which amalgamated *Vetus Latina*

---

[65] For a description, see ibid., pp. 259–60. [66] Ibid., p. 48.

[67] McGurk, 'The oldest manuscripts', 20.

[68] Houghton, *Latin New Testament*, pp. 55, 226. [69] Ibid., pp. 43, 50.

readings with Jerome's. While a good deal of such textual complexity is likely to have ensued from the vagaries of manuscript transmission, there were readers who set out to compare Latin translations. It was, no doubt, an inevitable stage in the Vulgate's path to dominance that the two competing traditions should have been regarded as commanding authority in concert.

Jerome's commission from Damasus was certainly an effective device in the pursuit of contemporary and later audiences. Although the extent to which this was so cannot be measured, a corpus of indirect signals shows that Jerome's emphases on Damasus' support yielded increasing dividends in the long run. For their relationship came to be seen as an archetype of what papal collaboration represented. The earliest known expression of that idealised reception are two letters about the liturgical use of the Psalter, purportedly exchanged between them. Damasus enquired and Jerome responded, as in their epistolary exchanges discussed above. The two forgeries have been dated roughly to the turn of the fifth century. They found application in Rome during the latter half of the 530s: the anonymous author of the *Liber pontificalis*, a collection of short papal biographies, used the letters as source material. In the ninth century, the letters were incorporated in the so-called Pseudo-Isidorian decretals, a great boon to their circulation.[70] It is also of significance that the decretals were a Frankish, rather than Roman, compilation, assembled for service in the heartlands of the Carolingian empire.[71] The incorporation of the forged exchange between Damasus and Jerome, therefore, testifies to perceptions north of the Alps. To return to the *Liber pontificalis*, it also introduced as a preface two new apocryphal letters between Jerome and Damasus. The actors in the roles of the one who requests and the one who complies were now reversed. Jerome asked for a chronological account of the deeds of all the popes from

---

[70] P. Blanchard, 'La correspondance apocryphe du pape S. Damase et de S. Jérôme sur le psautier et le chant de l'alleluia', *Ephemerides Liturgicae*, 63 (1949), 376–88, at 380–2.

[71] For previous scholarship and a fresh reading of the evidence, see E. Knibbs, 'Ebo of Reims, Pseudo-Isidore, and the Date of the False Decretals', *Speculum*, 92 (2017), 144–83.

St Peter to the present, to which the *Liber pontificalis* was the response.[72] The inversion of their functions in dialogue was necessary because the anonymous author of the *Liber pontificalis* held that Jerome was sojourning at Jerusalem during the period in question. Sources requisite for a papal chronology would not have been accessible there. A heavily edited text of a genuine letter by Jerome, *Ep.* 73, represents yet another variety of recasting and forgery. The redactor, who was a bad Latinist, apparently worked in the sixth century. The letter is concerned with the identify of Melchizedek, a biblical character. The original was addressed to Evangelus, and Pope Damasus was in no way involved. Disposing of Evangelus, the redactor-cum-forger relegated Jerome to recipient and attributed the letter to Damasus. The aim was apparently to stress that the opinions proposed in the letter were papal by definition.[73]

In medieval biographies, Jerome's Roman connexion is a recurrent feature.[74] The anonymous ninth-century author of the so-called 'Hieronymus noster', a hagiographic life, quoted the elegant first section of Damasus' final letter to Jerome, *Ep.* 35, discussed in Chapter 2.2.[75] Nicola Maniacutia, a twelfth-century biblical scholar, did the same in his life of Jerome.[76] As regards the translation of the Gospels, Nicola Maniacutia observed that Jerome had 'scrupulously corrected [their] text, confused at copyists' fault'.[77] The comment echoes the dedicatory letter to Damasus, prefacing the Gospels. All these notions were much in evidence in various types of writing concerning Jerome. Finally, John Beleth in his influential

---

[72] *Liber pontificalis*, ed. L. Duchesne, *Le Liber pontificalis: texte, introduction et commentaire*, 2 vols. (Paris: Thorin, 1886–92), vol. II, pp. 48–9, 117.

[73] J. Bignami-Odier, 'Une lettre apocryphe de saint Damase à saint Jérôme sur la question de Melchisédech', *Mélanges d'archéologie et d'histoire*, 63 (1951), 183–90. For other studies on forged exchanges between Jerome and Damasus, see Cain, *Letters of Jerome*, p. 67 n. 96.

[74] E. F. Rice, *Saint Jerome in the Renaissance* (Baltimore, ML: The Johns Hopkins University Press, 1985), pp. 23–48.

[75] 'Hieronymus noster', *PL*, 22, cols. 175–84, at 180–1.

[76] Nicola Maniacutia, *Vita S. Hieronymi*, *PL*, 22, cols. 183–202, at 188–9.

[77] Ibid., col. 189: 'Textum quatuor euangeliorum, scriptorum culpa confusum, diligenter correxit.'

treatise on liturgy, written in the 1160s, stated that Jerome reformed Catholic liturgy on the basis of a commission coming ultimately from Emperor Theodosius but assigned to him by Pope Damasus; that he corrected heterodox articulations of Origen's homilies read in Catholic services; that his biblical translations held the same authority as the Septuagint, the Greek Old Testament; and that Jerome served seven popes and was made the cardinal of San Lorenzo.[78] The office of cardinal priest was a medieval creation. A crude anachronism in a late-antique context, the designation was a conception of what Jerome's Roman standing should have been. The perception was ubiquitous and remained so for centuries. Countless medieval and early-modern visual representations, be they manuscript illustrations, wall-paintings or canvases, depict Jerome in a cardinal's red robes.

We may end with the visual evidence of a pictorial cycle found in two famous Carolingian bibles, which presents Jerome's career as a biblical translator and exegete. The manuscripts in question are the First Bible of Charles the Bald, now BnF, lat. 1, and the Bible of San Paolo fuori le mura in Rome. They date from 845 and the late 860s and come from Tours and Reims respectively.[79] Their Jerome illustrations comprise three panels.[80] In the first, Jerome leaves Rome to dedicate himself to biblical translation. The second panel shows him exposing the Bible to an audience of friends in Bethlehem. A stenographer beside him takes notes and scribes make further copies. In the third panel Jerome distributes copies of the Latin Bible to monks, who return to their communities, presumably in the Latin West. Costumes are Carolingian, but the narrative cycle, which must derive from a common source, is older, perhaps by centuries. At any rate, the second and

---

[78] John Beleth, *Summa de ecclesiasticis officiis*, 19, 57, 62, 106, 157, ed. H. Douteil, *CCCM*, 41A (1976), pp. 41–2, 103–4, 115, 197, 301 respectively.

[79] P. E. Dutton and H. L. Kessler, *The Poetry and Paintings of the First Bible of Charles the Bald* (Ann Arbor: The University of Michigan Press, 1997), p. 90 and J. E. Gaehde, 'The Bible of San Paolo fuori le mura in Rome and its date and its relation to Charles the Bald', *Gesta*, 5 (1966), 9–21.

[80] For reproductions, see Dutton and Kessler, *Poetry and Paintings*, Plate 5, and Gaehde, 'The Bible of San Paolo', 19, Plate 9 respectively.

third panels depict an early-medieval view of highly successful publication. The third panel, in which readers flock to Jerome to pick up copies, portrays mass production in contemporary terms. The scene is idealised and relates to circumstances in which the Vulgate was widely available. Even so, it does resonate with Jerome's experience after leaving Rome. In a letter written in the Holy Land *c*.392, he advised the recipient, Bishop Aurelius of Carthage, as follows.

> [A]s we have collated not a few things from sacred writings, should it please and suit you, you may do as your brothers, holy bishops from Gaul and Italy, have done and send someone you trust to be here for a year so that I can provide him with exemplars and he will bring to you all we have written. Latin scribes are not many in Jerusalem. Those two holy brothers whom I have as notaries can hardly keep pace with what I dictate.[81]

As in the Carolingian panels, Jerome had scribes to write down his words and parties from overseas came to obtain copies. He had established himself as a foremost Latin exegete, who published effectively far from many of his intended audiences. Papal patronage was no longer on offer or urgently needed. Yet Damasus' endorsement remained relevant, something made clear by the cited letter. Aurelius was informed that Jerome had translated two homilies by Origen on the *Song of Songs* on commission from Pope Damasus.[82]

---

[81] Jerome, *Ep.* 27*.3: 'Haec pauca de multis; ceterum quia orante te non parua de scripturis sanctis composuimus, si tibi placet et commodum uidetur, fac quod alii de Gallia et alii de Italia fratres tui, sancti episcopi, fecerunt, id est mitte aliquem fidum tibi qui unum annum hic faciat me exemplaria tribuente et deferat ad te cuncta quae scripsimus. Librariorum Latinorum Hierosolimae est penuria; nam ego duos sanctos fratres quos habeo notarios, uix queunt his quae dictamus occurrere.'

[82] Ibid., 27*.2.

3 Arator and Pope Vigilius

The first Latin author known to have dedicated a poem celebrating the papal office to the incumbent pope was Arator, subdeacon of a Roman church.[83] In the presbytery of St Peter's on Vatican Hill on 6 April 544, he presented Pope Vigilius with a copy of his new work, an epical rendition of the Acts of Apostles in hexameters, titled *Historia apostolica*. Several manuscripts of the work carry a short report of the event as a postscript, referred to here as *Relatio*.[84] The pope requested that extracts be read to the assembled party, which consisted of 'several bishops, presbyters, deacons and most of the clergy'. The reading completed, the pope ordered his chief of staff, Surgentius, to deposit the manuscript in the papal archives. Then 'all erudite students of literature' entreated the pope to arrange for Arator to read the whole work in public. A full recitation was staged at St Peter in Chains. The audience embraced 'a throng of churchmen as well as the lay nobility, and others even from the people' of Rome. The recitation took place over four days, 13 and 17 April and 8 and 30 May. The reception was enthusiastic: encores were repeatedly called for along the way.[85]

The recitations of the *Historia apostolica* at St Peter's and St Peter in Chains embody publication under papal auspices in a grand fashion. The affair has been described as 'the last attested "public reading" of a classical type'.[86] A contrasting view is that Arator's recitals were predominantly

---

[83] Haye, *Päpste und Poeten*, p. 113. For Arator's life, see Arator, *Historia apostolica*, English tr. R. Hillier (Liverpool University Press, 2020), 'Introduction', pp. 3–33 with abundant references.

[84] For the heading, see Arator, *Historia apostolica*, Relatio, ed. B. Bureau and P.-A. Deproost (Paris: Les Belles Lettres, 2017), p. 185.

[85] Ibid., pp. 185–6: 'plures episcopi, presbyteri, diacones et clerus pars maxima . . . litterati omnes doctissimi . . . religiosorum simul ac laicorum nobilium sed et e populo diuersorum turba conuenit'.

[86] H.-I. Marrou, review of *Aratoris subdiaconi De actibus apostolorum*, ed. McKinlay, *Gnomon*, 25 (1954), 253–5, at 255: 'la dernière "lecture publique" de type classique qui soit attestée'. See also T. Licht, '*Aratoris fortuna*: Zu Aufgang und Überlieferung der *Historia apostolica*', in A. Jördens, H. Gärtner, H. Görgemanns and A. Ritter, *Quaerite faciem eius semper. Studien zu den geistesgeschichtlichen Beziehungen zwischen*

representative of Pope Vigilius' policies.[87] What follows brings those views together. The two publication events will be assessed in relation to ancient traditions of public reading and contemporary political realities respectively.

The former event, the one arranged in the presbytery of St Peter's in April 544, is best understood in the framework of antique traditions of public reading. Reading one's own work aloud before an audience, an established practice in Greek antiquity, had been a feature of Rome's literary culture since the Augustan age. The works read on these occasions were to be published afterwards. Attendance was by invitation and for the upper social echelons. The imperial court was regularly involved. In as much as the audiences for recitations consisted of the *amici* of the event's organiser, they were a manifestation of Roman clientelism.[88] Those antique parameters help us appreciate the social function of the partial recitation of the *Historia apostolica* at St Peter's. With its party of priests under their supreme leader, the pope, the event exemplified papal clientelism. Although the setting was ecclesiastical, it echoed Rome's previous non-Christian literary traditions. Viewed from that perspective, the recitation can be understood as a demonstration of the papal assumption of the imperial persona.

The event was also seasoned with current ecclesiastical concerns. The date, 6 April, had significance. It has been observed that this was close to, but did not coincide with, the anniversary of Vigilius' papal ordination on 29 March; and that in 544 the annual celebration of his ordination had perhaps been postponed to allow for Easter festivities: Easter fell on 27 March that year.[89] What follows is a restatement of this argument with certain new observations. In sixth-century Rome, Easter Sunday was

Antike und Christentum. Dankesgabe für Albrecht Dihle aus dem Heidelberger Kirchenväterkolloquium (Hamburg: Kovac, 2008), pp. 163–79, at 163–4.

[87] C. Sotinel, 'Arator, un poète au service de la politique de Pape Vigile?', *Mélanges de l'École française de Rome*, 101 (1989), 805–20, esp. 806.

[88] F. Dupont, '*Recitatio* and the reorganization of the space of public discourse', in T. Habinek and A. Schiesaro (eds.), *The Roman Cultural Revolution* (Cambridge University Press, 1997), pp. 44–59.

[89] Sotinel, 'Arator, un poète', 816–17.

followed by seven so-called station (*statio*) days. On each day until Sunday, the pope performed a Mass, accompanied by a procession, in a prescribed church. On the anniversary of his papal ordination in 544, Vigilius was to officiate at St Paul's Outside the Walls (or, less likely, in some other church).[90] Such a liturgical obligation would have made the celebration of a papal anniversary unfeasible, or at least problematic. The papal anniversary was a grand occasion, to which the high clergy of neighbouring regions were invited and expected to come.[91] The festivity had become a stable tradition well before Vigilius' time, but if the incumbent so preferred, the timing could be adapted.[92] The day before the partial reading of the *Historia apostolica* to 'several bishops, presbyters, deacons and most of the clergy' at St Peter's was the octave of Vigilius' ordination. (An octave is the seventh day after a liturgical feast, on which the feast can be re-celebrated.) The attendance of bishops implies that invitees from neighbouring sees were present as they would have been at the celebration of a papal anniversary. It would have been impractical or impossible to mobilise (central) Italian high clergy to travel to Rome several times within a period of a few days. Rather, the audiences of the *Historia apostolica*'s first public reading and Vigilius' anniversary party were one.

In antique recitals, attendees were obliged to praise the author. The *Relatio* likewise reports that Arator's audience at St Peter's acclaimed his work. What constituted a departure from antique recitals, however, was that Arator presented a finished work. At least until the early imperial period, new works recited in public were expected to be late drafts, not quite finished in order that

[90] J. F. Baldovin, *The Urban Character of Christian Worship. The Origins, Development, and Meaning of Stational Liturgy* (Rome: Pont. Institutum Studiorum Orientalium, 1987), 147–53, 156–7.

[91] *Liber diurnus Romanorum pontificum ou Recueil des formules usitées par la chancellerie pontificale du Ve au XIe siècle*, ed. E. Rozière (Paris: Durand et Pedone-Lauriel, 1869), pp. 71–5.

[92] See, e.g., five sermons Leo I delivered on the anniversary of his papal *natalis*; *PL*, 54, cols. 141–56. In 591, Gregory I asked his clergy to come to celebrate his ordination not on the day of that anniversary, but on the *natalis* of St Peter; Gregory I, *Registrum epistularum*, i.39A, ed. P. Ewald and R. Hartmann, MGH, *Epistolae*, 1–2 (Berlin: Weidmann, 1891–9), vol. I, p. 54.

the audience could suggest final touches. But Arator's listeners still performed a literary critical function: they certified a clean copy with unpolluted text. According to *Relatio*, 'a codex like this was presented . . . by Arator . . . to Pope Vigilius, . . . and was received by him on 6 April in the presbytery of St Peter's', and was subsequently placed 'in the papal archives'.[93] The words 'codex like this' make the *Relatio* read as a *subscriptio*, a late-antique literary device.[94] Inserted at the end of a given work, a *subscriptio* announced that the under-signed party had amended its text. The party's official capacity and the date and place of the project's completion were often reported.[95] While *Relatio* differs from *subscriptiones* in its form, it communicates the same in its essence. The pope and his party attested that a copy with an accurate text had been received and would be preserved.

We may now turn to Arator's second recital, during which he read the *Historia apostolica* in full in instalments at St Peter in Chains on 13 and 17 April and 8 and 30 May. The event had apparently been premeditated while Arator was still writing, a suggestion which emerges from some verses of the text:

> Rome, it is by these very chains that your faith was strength-ened [and] your salvation was made eternal. Through their shackled bonds you will always be free. What could prevail over the chains that he who can absolve anything has touched? There is no enemy who can shatter these walls, invincible by virtue of his hand and pious triumph. The one who opens the door to stars closes the road to war.[96]

---

[93] Arator, *Historia apostolica*, Relatio, ed. Bureau and Deproost, pp. 185–6: 'oblatus est huiusmodi codex ab Aratore . . . papae Vigilio et susceptus ab eo die viii id. aprilis in presbiterio ante confessionem beati domni Petri . . . Quem cum ibidem legi mox pro aliqua parte fecisset, Surgentio . . . primicerio scholae notarium in scrinio dedit Ecclesiae collocandum'.

[94] Licht, '*Aratoris fortuna*', 164. [95] Cameron, *Last Pagans*, p. 493.

[96] Arator, *Historia apostolica*, i.1070–6: 'His solidata fides, his est tibi, Roma, catenis / perpetuata salus. Harum circumdata nexu / libera semper eris. Quid enim non uincula praestent / quae tetigit qui cuncta potest absoluere? Cuius / haec inuicta manu uel religiosa triumpho / moenia non ullo penitus quatientur ab hoste. / Claudit iter bellis qui portam pandit in astris.'

St Peter's chains were treasured and adored in the church where Arator recited his work. Repeating the Latin demonstrative determiner 'his' ('by these') within a single verse, the quotation's emphasis on them implies their immediacy. The verb 'tetigit' ('touched') may be construed as alluding to the same in a more indirect fashion. It should be noted how strategically this passage was located. It brings to a close Book 1, whose focus is on St Peter. (The hero of the second book is St Paul.) That Arator should have invoked the instruments of St Peter's martyrdom at hand and then paused his recital was a deliberate design to effect a thrilling climax.

The dramatic finale of Book 1 communicated a message of topical urgency. Although an epic whose subject matter was biblical, the work also incorporated comment on current affairs. An object of denunciation was the Arian heresy, entirely anachronistic to the times of Saints Peter and Paul. In its frequent Trinitarian and Christological reflexions and its condemnation of Anabaptism, the *Historia apostolica* contests Arius (†336), who is mentioned twice by name.[97] The subject held the utmost gravity. In the Gothic War of 535–54, Rome sided with Emperor Justinian's armies fighting the Ostrogoths, who were Arians. After the capture of Naples in 543, King Totila of the Ostrogoths turned his attention to Rome. The city stood in peril at the time of Arator's recital, and soon after, in 546 after a year-long siege, it was taken and pillaged by Totila's armies. Before the blockade, Totila had offered the Roman Senate favourable terms of surrender. When no capitulation came, he began a propaganda campaign targeted on the Roman population. A number of short missives were covertly carried into the town at night and set up in places where they would easily be seen in the morning. These open letters promised that no retaliation would fall on those who surrendered. The Roman leadership responded swiftly by expelling the Arian clergy, whom they suspected of collaboration with Totila's forces.[98] The two sides were in open competition for supporters within the city.

---

[97] Ibid., i.444 and 918. J. Schwind, *Arator-Studien* (Göttingen: Vandenhoeck & Ruprecht, 1990), pp. 215–20.

[98] Procopius, *History of the Wars*, vii.9, tr. H. Dewing, Loeb Classical Library, 5 vols. (Cambridge, MA: Harvard University Press, 1914–28), vol. IV, pp. 226–9.

Arator's assurances that no enemy could prevail over St Peter, Rome's protector, should be read as an effort to boost public morale in the face of the Gothic menace. To condemn Arianism was to rally against the Goths. These circumstances account for the egalitarianism of Arator's audience at St Peter in Chains, embracing plebeians as well as patricians. That sort of populistic element would have been unheard of in an antique literary party. The inclusive aspect of Arator's recital resonates with anti-Gothic preaching campaigns, such as Gregory Nazianzen's series of orations against Arianism in the wake of the Roman defeat at Adrianople in 378.[99] The four-day public reading at St Peter in Chains was, then, a literary event, a religious oration and a political rally. The two latter aspects were perhaps as important as the first. For, according to the *Relatio*, the audience requested several encores along the way. Arator's poetic devices, especially hyperbaton and recondite vocabulary, are a challenge for anyone without some serious grounding in Latin literature. One wonders how widely members of the audience, especially those representing the populace, were able to savour the literary finesse of what they heard.

The full recitation at St Peter in Chains was mandated by Pope Vigilius, who acted on the request of the 'erudite students of literature' present at the partial recitation at St Peter's according to *Relatio*.[100] However, as has been said, the odds are that the event had been envisaged even before the *Historia apostolica*'s completion. The pope was certainly involved in Arator's project even during its composition. Vigilius needed to muster support, and Arator's epic offered a means. Arator's order of subdeacon is a signal, previously unrecognised, which suggests that the work was in its entirety a papally provisioned undertaking. Before coming to Rome, Arator had served in the Gothic court as *comes domesticorum* and *comes priuatarum*.[101] The precise status of these positions remains unclear, but he had evidently been 'an official of great distinction'.[102] His Roman office of subdeacon was

---

[99] J. McGuckin, *St. Gregory of Nazianzus: An Intellectual Biography* (New York: St Vladimir's Seminary Press, 2001), pp. 233–240.

[100] See n. 85 above.

[101] Arator, *Historia apostolica*, Relatio, ed. Bureau and Deproos, p. 185.

[102] R. P. H. Green, *Latin Epics of the New Testament: Juvencus, Sedulius, Arator* (Oxford University Press, 2006), p. 257.

low-ranking for a man with such credentials. Also his excellent education, remarkable networks and the pomp and circumstance of the *Historia apostolica*'s publication are indicative of some social dignity. The discrepancy between his middling formal status at Rome and the elevated status detectable elsewhere calls for explanation. It is significant that the office of subdeacon was connected to the production of martyr histories at Rome.[103] Subdeacons supervised notaries assigned to write down the acts of martyrs. The evidence of that comes from the *Liber pontificalis*, a collection of short papal biographies drawn up at Rome, mentioned above in Chapter 2.3. The first recension of the *Liber pontificalis* was composed soon after the incumbency of Pope Agapetus in 535–6, at about the time Arator came to Rome.[104] The biographical note on Pope Fabian I, which belongs to this first recension, states that Fabian 'created seven subdeacons who were to supervise seven notaries, so that [the latter] would accurately put together the complete acts of martyrs'.[105] It has recently been proposed that in the sixth century four *gesta martyrum*, or deeds of the martyrs, were composed under this system at Rome.[106] The reporting of miracles and martyrdoms, always done in a straightforward manner and in plain style, contrasted with Arator's epic register. But in its chronicling of the deeds of Saints Peter and Paul, the *Historia apostolica* is a *gesta martyrum* none the less. It may also be noted that Arator had toyed with the notion of composing a biblical poem for years. But it was only after his entry into papal service that he chose to focus on Peter and Paul, two Christian martyrs.[107]

Papal involvement shows through. Arator prefixed to his work a dedicatory letter to his master, Pope Vigilius. It opens as follows.

---

[103] I owe this observation to Dr Andrea Verardi.

[104] R. McKitterick, *Rome and the Invention of the Papacy: The* Liber Pontificalis (Cambridge University Press, 2020), p. 12.

[105] *Liber pontificalis*, xxi.2, ed. Duchesne, vol. II, p. 148: 'Hic regiones diuidit diaconibus et fecit VII subdiaconos qui VII notariis inminerent, ut gestas martyrum integro fideliter colligerent.'

[106] A. Verardi, *La memoria legittimante: Il* Liber pontificalis *e la chiesa di Roma del secolo VI* (Rome: ISIME, 2016), pp. 151–3.

[107] Arator, *Historia apostolica, Ep. ad Parthenium*, 53–82.

As I hand over this gift of love to you, great father, consider
that I repay a debt owed to your merits. I am a recruit under
your guidance; I learn the doctrine with you as my teacher.
If anything from my lips is pleasing, praise will belong to the
guide.[108]

That acknowledgement is much to the fore in Arator's overarching
emphasis on Petrine primacy. St Peter occupies a considerably more
prominent role in the *Historia apostolica* than in the Book of Acts.
According to a modern commentator, Arator's Peter is something almost
of a god dwelling on earth.[109] The subject had topicality in the 540s.
Emperor Justinian's vigorous ecclesiastical policies, of which the so-called
Three-Chapters Controversy was a prime instance, threatened papal primacy as it had been conceived by Damasus.[110] Accordingly, the final
chapter of the *Historia apostolica* stresses that 'Peter arose as the commander
in the body of the church' and that 'every throne pays attention to the robust
heights of the mistress of the whole world'.[111]

3.1 The Impact

The recital at St Peter in Chains had a long-term impact at the scene.
Evidence for that is found in the so-called *Corpus Laureshamense*,
a composite manuscript, now BAV, Pal. lat. 833, in which are assembled
epigraphic collections from various sources, put together sometime before
*c.*835 at Lorsch in central Germany.[112] One of its components reports

---

[108] Ibid., *Ep. ad Vigilium*, 27–30: 'Hoc tibi, magne pater, cum defero munus
amoris, / respice quod meritis debita soluo tuis. / Te duce tiro legor, te dogmata
disco magistro. / Si quid ab ore placet, laus monitoris erit.'

[109] Schwind, *Arator-Studien*, p. 83.

[110] R. Hillier, *Arator on the Acts of the Apostoles: A Baptismal Commentary* (Oxford:
Clarendon Press, 1993), pp. 3–4.

[111] Arator, *Historia apostolica*, ii.1225–8: 'Petrus in ecclesiae surrexit corpore
princeps . . . speculetur ut omnis / terrarum dominae fundata cacumina sedes.'

[112] *ICUR*, vol. II, pp. 95–7 and C. V. Franklin, 'The epigraphic *syllogae* of BAV,
Palatinus Latinus 833', in J. Hamesse (ed.), *Roma, magistra mundi. Itineraria*

a sequence of four epigraphs, of which the first two quote Arator and the following two patently came from St Peter in Chains. Ignored in previous scholarship on the reception of Arator, their status may be briefly assessed here. We may begin with the inscriptions certainly from St Peter in Chains. One records the fulfilment of a vow of Eudoxia, her father Theodosius and his wife Eudoxia. These were Eudoxia († *c.*493), who was the consort of Emperor Valentinian III and who provided funds to rebuild the destroyed church, and her parents, Emperor Theodosius II and Empress Eudoxia. Although the epigraph does not identify the vow, it must have embraced her sponsorship of the work of reconstruction.[113] The other inscription patently from St Peter in Chains commemorates Pope Sixtus III (†440) and Presbyter Philip, who, respectively, dedicated the basilica and supervised the project of reconstruction.[114] As for the two immediately preceding Arator inscriptions, they are associated with St Peter in Chains on account of his publication of the *Historia apostolica* there. Furthermore, the subject matter of the first epigraph is the above-quoted celebration of Peter's chains, with which Book 1 concludes.[115] The second Arator epigraph is discussed shortly. The four inscriptions constitute a discrete whole by virtue of their shared associations with St Peter in Chains.[116] It is highly unlikely

culturae medievalis. Mélanges offert au Père L.E. Boyle à l'occasion de son 75e anniversaire, 3 vols. (Louvain-la-Neuve: FIDEM, 1998), vol. II, pp. 975–90.

[113] *ICUR*, vol. II, p. 110 no. 66

[114] Ibid., no. 67. The inscription is also recorded in another manuscript, which explicitly identifies it as belonging to St Peter in Chains, ibid., p. 134. Mounted in 1931, the epigram is found again in the church; T. Lansford, *The Latin Inscriptions of Rome: A Walking Guide* (Baltimore, ML: The Johns Hopkins University Press, 2009), p. 105 n. e.

[115] *ICUR*, vol. II, p. 110, no. 64.

[116] De Rossi (ibid., pp. 110–11 no. 68) proposed that a fifth epigraph, immediately following the one about Pope Sixtus and Presbyter Philip in the said manuscript, is likewise from St Peter in Chains, arguing that it served as a legend for a depiction of the martyrdom of St Paul, the church's original patron together with St Peter. The case is less solid, however. Two inscriptions of unknown origin follow this epigraph on St Paul, for which reason all three may derive from the same unidentifiable location.

that a copyist, of the *Corpus Laureshamense* or a lost intermediate source, would have brought them together from various sources. To do so, he would have to have known that the church had previously been dedicated to Saints Peter and Paul, as in the Sixtus epigraph; that the vow of Eudoxia and her parents concerned that same church, not identified in the inscription in question; and that Arator had recited his work there. The manuscript received the epigraphs, probably through an intermediate source, from notes taken on the spot in the seventh century or even the sixth.[117]

The second Arator epigraph reads: 'The eunuch's profuse faith was immediately incited by the sight of water; baptised, he is in peace.'[118] The context is Acts 8:26–40, the baptism of the Ethiopian Eunuch by Philip the Evangelist. Extracted from a longer sentence, the epigraph was slightly modified to make a coherent whole and, no doubt, to explain the painting to which it served as a legend.[119] Contrasting with Philip's several appearances in Acts, in the *Historia apostolica* he only features in the story in question. To spot the verse, the party responsible for the inscription must have known Arator's epic rather well.

While the recitation at St Peter in Chains was a great success critically, to judge by the testimony of the *Relatio*, the venue seems to have served in other respects as an ideal setting for publication. It was clear that in a foreseeable future, pilgrims would flock there to commemorate the instruments of Peter's martyrdom, a tangible connexion to Arator's subject matter. Among them, many would be literate and some would acquire books. What better advertisement for an epic on St Peter's martyrdom could there be than to have its verses inscribed on the very walls that enclosed his chains? Early manuscripts of the *Historia apostolica* do not survive from Rome, an absence of evidence rather than evidence of absence. Interestingly, one setting for commercial book dissemination stood in the immediate proximity to St Peter in Chains: the bookshop of a certain Gaudiosus was situated adjacent to the church. The evidence comes from

---

[117] *ICUR*, vol. II, pp. 97 and 111 n. 68.

[118] Ibid., p. 110, no. 65: 'Conspectis properanter aquis ardescere cepit / eunuchi fecunda fides quiescit emersus.'

[119] Arator, *Historia apoastolica*, i.687–90.

a colophon in a late ninth-century copy of the Gospels, now Angers, BM, MS 24 (20). According to the colophon, 'Gaudiosus' bookshop', *statio Gaudiosi librarii*, had produced a copy of Jerome's translation of the Gospels; this would have been an exemplar from which the Angers manuscript descended, perhaps through an intermediary. The colophon resembles others from late antiquity.[120] The need to identify the translation as Jerome's at Rome suggests, according to one of today's most authoritative specialists, that the lost ancestor of the Angers manuscript dated from the sixth century at the latest.[121] Bookshops disappeared from Rome after the Gothic devastation of 546, for which reason it has been argued that Gaudiosus' was still operative on the occasion of Arator's recital.[122]

The success of Arator's work cannot, of course, be explained by appeal to political motifs, authorial recitations and the infrastructure of bookmaking in Rome. The former only amounted to a subsidiary theme, while the deeds of Peter and Paul, a subject of universal Christian relevance, supply the leitmotif. Arator wrote with wider readerships in mind.[123] He consigned the work to two associates, Parthenius and Florianus. His dedicatory letter to Florianus makes no mention of the papacy, for which reason the case is introduced here only briefly. Florianus, an abbot, is an elusive figure. He may have been the abbot of 'Romenum' either near Milan or closer to Trento, or of Romainmôtier in today's Switzerland. He was apparently the same Florianus who received two letters from Ennodius, a bishop and poet, who had mentored the young Arator.[124] A short *accessus* to Arator, a biographical note on him, found in several Carolingian

[120] D. De Bruyne, 'Gaudiosus, un vieux libraire romain', *Revue Bénédictine*, 30 (1913), 343–5.

[121] P.-M. Bogaert, 'The Latin Bible', in J. Carleton Paget and J. Schaper (eds.), *The New Cambridge History of the Bible. I. From the Beginnings to 600* (Cambridge University Press, 2013), pp. 505–26, at 519.

[122] P. Supino Martini, 'Aspetti della cultura grafica a Roma fra Gregorio Magno e Gregorio VII', in *Roma nell'alto medievo*, 2 vols. (Spoleto: CISAM, 2001), vol. II, pp. 911–68, at 925–6.

[123] Arator, *Historia apostolica*, i.404 and ii.995–7.

[124] Arator, *Historia apostolica*, English tr. Hillier, p. 225 n. 629; Schwind, *Arator-Studien*, p. 10 n. 5; Green, *Latin Epics*, pp. 263–4.

manuscripts, proposes that Florianus was given the work so that the 'volume would be reinforced by means of his authority'.[125] This is no doubt true in respect of local transmission. It resonates with Arator's depiction of Florianus as an avid reader with access to a great number of books.[126] The implication is that Florianus presided over a community with an impressive library, and Arator sought to have his work installed there.

As for his other dedicatee outside Rome, Parthenius was approached so that readerships in Gaul could be accessed. Parthenius, with whom Arator had studied as a young man, was a *magister officiorum* in the court of King Theudebert I of Austrasia. The man was a scion of a well-connected senatorial family in Gaul. He was apparently a nephew of Ennodius, the said patron of the young Arator.[127] In a dedicatory letter attached to, or sent with, the copy consigned to Parthenius, Arator praised his friend as renowned for erudition in Germania.[128] The aspect of learning was important because Arator requested that Parthenius use his connexions to promote the poem among bishops in 'learned Gaul' (*Gallia studiosa*), 'for they are teachers of faith'.[129] This and what would be the phenomenal subsequent dissemination of the *Historia apostolica* as a Latin textbook suggest that Arator's objective was to penetrate Gaulish classrooms by means of episcopal influence. Efforts to supersede pagan literature with Christian poetry at schools were in evidence across Christendom, from fourth-century Constantinople to eighth-century Northumbria.[130] Gregory

---

[125] 'Scripsit hanc epistolam ad Florianum abbatem, ut sua auctoritate roboraretur uolumen eius'; e.g. BnF, lat. 2773 and 8095.

[126] Arator, *Historia apostolica*, *Ep. ad Florianum*, 9–10: 'Inter grandiloquos per mille uolumina libros, / maxima cum teneas et breuiora lege.'

[127] B. Bureau, 'Parthenius et la question de l'authenticité de la Lettre à Parthenius d'Arator', in B. Bureau and C. Nicolas (eds.), *Moussyllanea. Mélanges de linguistique et de littérature anciennes offerts à Claude Moussy* (Leuven: Peeters, 1998), pp. 387–97.

[128] Arator, *Historia apostolica*, *Ep. ad Parthenium*, 15 (and 37–48).

[129] Ibid., 91: 'sunt quia pontifices in religione magistri'.

[130] S. Heikkinen, 'The Christianization of Latin metre: a study of Bede's *De arte metrica*', unpublished PhD dissertation (University of Helsinki, 2012), pp. 4, 9–11, and passim.

Nazianzen's poem *To his own verses* (Εἰς τὰ ἔμμετρα, *In suos versus*) may be instanced here as testament to such aspirations.

> I wished to present my work to the young people – and especially those who enjoy literature – as a kind of pleasant medicine, as inducement which might lead them to more useful things ... I cannot allow that the pagans should have greater literary talent than us. I am speaking of those ornate words of theirs, for in our eyes beauty lies in contemplation.[131]

The period of Arator's active years saw several attempts to foster Christian literary education. The onus of implementation was on bishops, as stated in the pertinent stipulations of an ecclesiastical assembly in Provence in 529 and the second council of Toledo in 531.[132] On the evidence of Venantius Fortunatus' *Vita sancti Martini*, it has been argued that Arator's verse had already been incorporated into a school curriculum within some twenty years of its publication. This work, written apparently at Poitiers sometime between 573 and 576, sings the praises of Arator, mentioning him by name. Venantius, who was born near Treviso in the 530s and studied in Ravenna in the 550s or 560s, would have read Arator during his school years in northern Italy.[133] Be that as it may, a group of late ancient Christian poets, Arator, Juvencus, Sedulius and Prudentius, had widely replaced in grammatical education

---

[131] Gregory Nazianzen, *Carmina moralia*, *Patrologia Graeca*, 37 (Paris: Apud J.-P. Migne, 1862), cols. 397–1600, at 1331–2; tr. A. Usacheva, *Knowledge, Language and Intellection from Origen to Gregory Nazianzen. A Selective Survey* (Frankfurt am Main: Peter Lang, 2017), pp. 36–7.

[132] J. Fontaine, 'Education and learning', in P. Fouracre (ed.), *The New Cambridge Medieval History*, I: c.*500*–c.*700* (Cambridge University Press, 2005), pp. 735–59, at 744.

[133] Venantius Fortunatus, *Vita sancti Martini*, i.22–23, ed. S. Quesnel (Paris: Les Belles Lettres, 1996), p. 7 and 'Introduction', p. xv; B. Brennan, 'The career of Venantius Fortunatus', *Traditio*, 41 (1985), 49–78, at 67, 71.

the pagan classics, with the exception of Virgil, by the end of the seventh century.[134]

Arator used the pope's endorsement as bait. In his dedicatory letter to Parthenius, he mentioned that Pope Vigilius had ordered the work's preservation in the papal library, a plain allusion to the *Relatio*. Asserting that the learned circles of Gaul would certainly appreciate a piece commended by the pope, he pointed out that Parthenius would obtain fame by circulating the *Historia apostolica*.[135] Arator's affirmations bespeak a conviction that papal engagement in publication would advance dissemination far from Rome. Such confidence was apparently well founded. Arator's most recent editors argue on the basis of textual evidence that the earliest phase of its transmission now traceable through manuscripts in all probability derives ultimately from Parthenius' now lost copy.[136] If so, that volume fathered numerous offspring; our earliest complete manuscripts, which are from the ninth century, descend from it. Interestingly, the dedicatory letter to Parthenius is found in only two of the nine copies that represent the earliest stratum of the tradition.[137] These are BnF, lat. 2773 and 9347, both from the same centre of Reims. Parthenius died in 548, granting him approximately four years to promote the *Historia apostolica*. A paucity of time, however, can hardly account for the insignificant transmission of the letter to him. For, once incorporated in a copy of the *Historia apostolica*, the letter would have been transmitted to new copies if the scribes responsible for them so decided. Many obviously preferred not to. This may have had to do with Parthenius' poor reputation: he was lynched by a mob angered by the crown's fiscal policies, for which he was blamed. In the eyes of contemporaries, his terrible death was fair retribution for his sins. Gregory of Tours (†594) dedicated a short vignette to Parthenius in his very influential history of the Franks. Gregory's Parthenius was a glutton, who broke wind in public, and had his wife and friend killed when he wrongly suspected them

---

[134] P. Riché, *Éducation et culture dans l'occident barbare, VIe–VIIIe siècles* (Paris: Seuil, 1962), pp. 121–39.

[135] Arator, *Historia apostolica, Ep. ad Parthenium*, 87–8, 97–100.

[136] Ibid., ed. Bureau and Deproost, 'Introduction', pp. cvii–cviii, cxxx–cxxxi.

[137] This figure excludes the two earliest copies, of which only fragments survive.

of adultery.[138] The man was destined to posthumous neglect. The reduced transmission of Arator's letter to him contrasts with the dissemination of both the dedicatory letter to Pope Vigilius and the *Relatio*, the report of the publication event in Rome. The former is included in each of the nine early manuscripts, and seven of them also carry the *Relatio*.[139]

The *Relatio* was certainly communicated to Gaul in the copy Arator sent to Parthenius. The evidence of our earliest complete manuscripts and the aforementioned allusion to *Relatio* in the dedicatory letter to Parthenius combines to suggest this was so.[140] To that extent, *Relatio* reads not only as a postscript with a text-critical function resembling that of a *subscriptio*, but also as a promotional piece. Arator may have penned it, for he certainly took benefit in advertising the papal endorsement. Be that as it may, the contrast between the transmission of the *Historia apostolica*'s papal paratexts and that of the dedicatory letter to Parthenius hints that it was the association of the former, and not the latter, that gave the boost to the work's dissemination in Gaul.

---

[138] Gregory of Tours, *Libri historiarum X*, iii.36, ed. B. Krusch and W. Levison, MGH, *Scriptores rerum Merovingicarum*, 1 (Hanover: Hahn, 1951), pp. 131–2.

[139] Arator, *Historia apostolica*, ed. Bureau and Deproost, 'Introduction', pp. cxiv–cxxii.

[140] Ibid., pp. cxxx–cxxxi.

4 Fulcoius of Beauvais and Pope Alexander II

Fulcoius of Beauvais was a poet who flourished in northern France in the final third of the eleventh century and, it would seem, somewhat later. A man who has scarcely featured in modern scholarship, he requires a brief introduction. Details about his life, which are few, testify to an eventful ecclesiastical career. Fulcoius was born at Beauvais and educated at Meaux. He was recruited to the administration of Archbishop Manasses I of Reims (*sedit*, 1069–80) apparently by 1070.[141] In that capacity, he visited Rome in 1073 at the latest, where he presented to the pope his chief literary work, a long biblical epic called *De nuptiis Christi et ecclesiae* ('On the Marriage of Christ and the Church'). It is the implications of that event that are the subject of this chapter. Archbishop Manasses' own career ended in disgrace. Accused of simony and repeated violations against his own clergy, he persistently defied the efforts of Hugh of Die, papal legate to France, to adjudicate on his case. Hugh had Manasses excommunicated and deposed in the Council of Lyon in 1080, which sentences Pope Gregory VII confirmed later that year.[142] Manasses' last appearance in the historical record is in the camp of King Henry IV of Germany before Rome the next year.[143] Fulcoius, a propagandist for Manasses and member of his episcopal *familia*, had followed him there.[144] With his patron

---

[141] *Recueil des actes de Philippe Ier*, ed. M. Prou (Paris: Imprimerie Nationale, 1908), nos. 48 and 49, pp. 131–4.

[142] K. R. Rennie, *Law and Practice in the Age of Reform. The Legatine Work of Hugh of Die (1073–1106)* (Turnhout: Brepols, 2010), pp. 134–41.

[143] J. R. Williams, 'Manasses I of Rheims and Pope Gregory VII', *American Historical Review*, 54 (1949), 804–24, at 806–12, 820, 823.

[144] Fulcoius addressed a versified letter to Henry IV, in which Henry is said to be approaching Rome, as he was in Spring 1081; Fulcoius, *Epistulae*, 1, ed. M. L. Colker in *Traditio*, 10 (1954), 191–273, at 208: 'Non nouus accedis Romae, rex, indolis haeres perstas Romanae, solii sicut speciei heres ut generis non degenerando triumphi.' A. Boutémy, 'Essai de chronologie des poésies de Foulcoie de Beauvais', *Annuaire de l'Institut de philologie et d'histoire orientales et slaves*, 11 (1951), 79–96, at 88–90 dates the letter to 1084 on account of Henry's designation as 'Cesar' at its beginning. However, in 1081 Henry made known that he came to Rome to claim the imperial title, a condition implied in the

unseated, he would have felt uncertain of his professional future; he offered to compose poems in honour of Henry IV.[145] The proposal was rejected, as can be deduced from the absence of any such writings in his corpus and from the path of his subsequent career.

Fulcoius's journey with Manasses in 1081 was apparently referred to *c.*1097 in a letter of Bruno of Cologne, the founder of the Carthusian order and previously a dignitary at Reims. The letter exhorts the addressee, Raoul the Verd, provost and future archbishop of Reims, to fulfil the promise he had once made to enter religion. Raoul had made that commitment together with Bruno and Fulcoius ('Fulcuius') at Reims. Their plan was to execute their pledge together after Fulcoius' journey to Rome in the archbishop's entourage, then impending. When his return was postponed, Raoul failed to take the promised step. To judge by the timing of Bruno's own entry to religion, the affair took place probably in 1081.[146] Fulcoius' frustrated promises and futile quest for foreign patronage in that year were, no doubt, side-effects of his patron's adversities. To make matters worse, in December 1080, the pope had commanded that the clergy of Reims should 'not share in [Manasses'] perverse deeds such that he be removed from [their] midst and that [they] in every way resist him'.[147] The clerk of an ousted prelate, Fulcoius saw his prospects vanish. What is more, the pope's injunction was certainly a source also of spiritual pressure for those who served Manasses. Fulcoius' pledge to take the monastic vow, subsequently forsaken, perhaps resulted from such fears.

quotation above; I. S. Robinson, *Henry IV of Germany 1056–1106* (Cambridge University Press, 1999), p. 213. Fulcoius referred also to Pope Alexander as 'Caesar'; Fulcoius Belvacensis, *Vtriusque de nuptiis Christi et ecclesiae libri septem*, 'Versus papae Alexandro et Hyldebranno archidiacono', ed. M. I. J. Rousseau (Washington, DC: The Catholic University of America Press, 1960), p. 2*.

[145] Fulcoius, *Ep.* 1, ed. Colker, pp. 211–12.

[146] A. Wilmart, 'Deux lettres concernant Raoul le Verd, l'ami de saint Bruno', *Revue Bénédictine*, 51 (1939), 257–74, at 264, 268.

[147] Gregory VII, *Registrum*, viii.17, ed. E. Caspar, MGH, *Epistolae selectae*, 2, 2nd ed., 2 vols. (Berlin: Weidmann, 1955), p. 539: 'Quapropter apostolica uos auctoritate monemus, ut peruersis actibus eius in nullo communicetis, immo ut tollatur de medio uestrum et . . . sibi modis omnibus resistatis.'

Fulcoius was able to return to the chapter of Reims at an unknown point of time. Archdeacon Wido of Reims, who had belonged to Manasses' supporters, may have been instrumental; Fulcoius celebrated his patronage in a letter, which is, unfortunately, undatable.[148] Be that as it may, even before his exile with Manasses, he could mingle with the archbishop's enemies in Reims, of whom the above-mentioned Bruno was one. Fulcoius is attested as a subdeacon in Reims in 1093.[149] One of the signatories to a Reims charter of 1097 is a Fulcoius, named without designation; but given the name's rarity, this must have been our man.[150] The document makes it clear that he did not hold office among the highest-ranking members of the chapter. The attestations appear in the hierarchical order of office, from the archbishop to the chancellor, after whom are named the rest without indication of precedence, including our poet. The odds are that Fulcoius was still a subdeacon. He was, however, one of the canons of the cathedral chapter and may have enjoyed income from one or more prebends.[151] What is more, a man named Fulco attested several charters between 1086 and 1119; his designation was subdeacon up to and including a 1096 charter, and deacon in an 1102 charter and thereafter.[152] In principle, the names Fulco and Fulcoius should not be equated, but medieval spelling of names was flexible in general. An 1119 charter's witnesses included Fulcuinus, a deacon.[153] Because the subdeacons and deacons of Reims were relatively small groups of men, and Fulco, Fulcuinus and Fulcoius never appear in the same witness list, I am inclined to identify them as one. In other words, Fulcoius would have been promoted, but only after the incumbency of Archbishop Renaud, Manasses' successor. Although permitted back into the fold, Fulcoius was not part of the inner circle before Renaud's death in 1096. The same impression is gained from his surviving works, which are silent about Manasses' successors,

---

[148] Fulcoius, *Ep.* 10, ed. Colker, p. 247; Williams, 'Manasses I', 810.

[149] Châlons-en-Champagne, AD Marne, 13 H 72 n° 1.

[150] Reims, AD Marne, 57 H 1.

[151] Ibid., 56 H 525 begins 'De canonicis Sanctae Mariae', and then follow officeholders, of whom subdeacons are named last.

[152] Ibid., 56 H 980 and 56 H 268 respectively.   [153] Ibid., 2 G 2158 n° 1.

suggesting an absence of effective patronage. After 1119, we lose sight of Fulcoius other than that he is known to have been buried in Meaux.[154] He is, therefore, likely also to have gained some preferment to the Meaux chapter. This would resonate with the fact that roughly one half of his hagiographical writings concern the patron saints of houses in that diocese.[155] A comparable geographical focus does not emerge from the rest of the corpus. A fourteenth-century cartulary of Meaux recites an 1107 charter with the attestation 'Fulgonis archidiaconi'.[156] The above-mentioned quandary applies here; the spelling suggests the name Fulco rather than Fulcoius. The reference has previously been accepted as evidencing Fulcoius, however; for external evidence from manuscript rubrics to his works designate him invariably as archdeacon of an undesignated diocese and as subdeacon of Meaux.[157] Fulcoius would, then, have ended his career in a senior position holding canonries in plurality, at Reims and Meaux. The year of his death is unknown.[158]

The corpus of Fulcoius' extant pieces embraces letters, epitaphs, *nugae* or light-hearted poems and a biblical epic. All are verse, most often hexameters. The poetic nature of his writings in most cases defies efforts to date them with firm termini. For instance, one cannot be sure whether all his letters were carried to their addressees or composed exclusively for publication in a collection. If his letter to Archbishop Gervais of Reims was an authentic missive, it was sent sometime before the conclusion of the latter's incumbency in 1067.[159] The implication would be that patronage

---

[154] Fulcoius, *De nuptiis*, ed. Rousseau, 'Appendix II', p. 125.

[155] *Vita S. Agili*, *Vita S. Faronis* and *Vita S. Blandini*; for a list of his hagiographical pieces, see ibid., pp. 35–6.

[156] Meaux, BM, MS 63, p. 17.

[157] For the manuscript rubrics, see Fulcoius, *De nuptiis*, ed. Rousseau, 'Introduction', pp. 1 n. 4, and 22. J. S. Ott, '"Rome and Reims are equals": Archbishop Manasses I (*c.* 1069–80), Pope Gregory VII, and the fortunes of historical exceptionalism', in S. Danielson and E. A. Gatti (eds.), *Envisioning the Bishop: Images and the Episcopacy in the Middle Ages* (Turnhout: Brepols, 2014), pp. 275–302, at 281 n. 21.

[158] Cf. Wilmart, 'Foulcoie, itinéraire', 52 n. 77.

[159] Fulcoius, *Ep.* 18, ed. Colker, pp. 253–6.

was sought from Reims even before Manasses' elevation to the archbish-opric. Two epitaphs in honour of Queen Matilda of England, who died in 1083, are the latest of Fulcoius' compositions to which a watertight *terminus post quem* can be affixed.[160] Several of his other pieces are likely to be later, quite possibly by several years. While much of Fulcouis and his career remains a mystery, the pool of biographical details and his extant composi-tions are suggestive of a man whose authorial career survived but suffered from his alliance with a disgraced patron. What follows seeks to understand the ambitions he had for *De nuptiis Christi et ecclesiae*, his *magnum opus*, and explain his failure to realise them through planned recourse to the papacy.

4.1 A Presentation at Rome

Fulcoius completed *De nuptiis Christi et ecclesiae*, henceforth *De nuptiis*, sometime between 1069 and April 1073, during his first years under Manasses' service. A long biblical epic in hexameter verse, it belongs to the same genre as Arator's *Historia apostolica*. It is a work of considerable literary ambition. Running to 4,737 lines, its narrative extends from Genesis to the Acts of the Apostles, a scope that exceeds that of late-antique biblical epicists, including Arator. Composition must have taken years. For instance, Lawrence of Durham, a twelfth-century versifier of the Bible, wrote 3,076 lines of non-rhyming elegiac couplets in a period of three to four years.[161] Fulcoius is likely to have begun *De nuptiis* before relocating to Reims *c.*1070. At the time of completion he enjoyed Manasses' patronage, as the poem makes abundantly clear on multiple occasions.[162]

De nuptiis survives in three twelfth-century manuscripts, to be discussed in due course. One, BnF, lat. 16701, prefaces the text with a verse address to Pope Alexander II and Archdeacon Hildebrand, a zealous reformer and the future Pope Gregory VII. The final terminus for publication, April 1073, is supplied by Pope Alexander's death. The poem first laments the demise of Rome's past glories and then celebrates her new heroes, Alexander and

---

[160] Ibid., 'Introduction', p. 193.

[161] Lawrence of Durham, *Hypognosticon*, Prologus, in *Dialogi Laurentii Dunelmensis monachi ac prioris*, ed. J. Raine, Surtees Society, 70 (1880), p. 64.

[162] Fulcoius, *De nuptiis*, i.11–12, i.134–5, vii.1300–7, and apparently vii.1451–4.

Hildebrand. Its peroration communicates the presentation to them of a copy of *De nuptiis* and offers compliments to Manasses:

> As it is not honourable to have seen them [Pope Alexander and Hildebrand] with empty hands – for I know that poems pleased Roman gods – I carry poems, desirable articles to such great patrons. During the times of the learned pope and [his] worthy minister, at the instigation of Manasses, a very worthy lover of poetry, under the guidance of the sacred master, who gives the understanding of word, who embraces the world, I have put together the Old and the New Testament here, the reading of which will be instructive.[163]

The articulations 'hos uiduisse' ('to have seen them') and 'deporto' ('I carry') imply Fulcoius' own agency in presenting the copy. That reading finds support in his later remark that he had crossed the Alps on Manasses' order.[164] Because the presentation cannot be dated other than as 1069 × 1073, its implications in respect of Manasses are not entirely clear. If the date was towards the beginning of that timeframe, the objective would have been to thank the pope and his preeminent servant for favouring Manasses' election.[165] A later date would instead connect the event to negotiations about a vacancy after the death of Abbot Herimar of Saint-Remi in 1071, which Manasses was reluctant to fill.[166] Either way, Fulcoius promoted the archbishop in the papal court.[167] He did the same in epistolary poems

---

[163] Ibid., 'Versus Alexandro et Hyldebranno', 17–24: 'Hos uacua uidisse manu cum non sit honestum, / Romanis placuisse deis quia carmina noui, / Carmina deporto tantis optanda patronis. / Temporibus docti papae dignique ministri, / Instinctu Manasae condigni carmen amantis, / Hic testamentum, sacro monstrante magistro, / Qui dat noticiam uocis, qui continet orbem, / Composui uetus atque nouum, quae lecta docebunt.' I have slightly amended the punctuation.

[164] Fulcoius, *Ep.* 26, lines 57–9, ed. Colker, p. 268; see also *Ep.* 7.

[165] Ott, 'Rome and Reims are equals', 282. [166] Williams, 'Manasses I', 808.

[167] M. L. Colker, 'Fulcoius of Beauvais, poet and propagandist', in M. W. Herren, C. J. McDonough and R. G. Arthur (eds.), *Latin Culture in the Eleventh Century:*

addressed to Pope Alexander II in the early 1070s and, some years later, to Pope Gregory VII, and to Hugh of Die, the said papal legate to France.[168]

It should be emphasised that *De nuptiis* must not be regarded exclusively, or even primarily, as a publicity campaign for Archbishop Manasses. A literary patron's task was to enable the authorial process, for which the reward was fame.[169] The work, not the patron, was at the centre. That applies in the case of *De nuptiis*. A long versification of the Christian salvation history, it exudes aspirations that surpass its panegyrical function. A comparison to Arator is again instructive. The *Historia apostolica* was, at one level, a propaganda piece in service of Arator's patron, Pope Vigilius. But in reaching for audiences far from Rome, Arator saw his work in a wider setting than just service to the papal cause. A letter by which Fulcoius subsequently dedicated a collection of shorter verse to Manasses implies that he likewise regarded his work as transcending the service it paid the patron. A panegyric celebrating Manasses' maecenate, the letter argues that Reims rivalled Rome. To make that case, Fulcoius adduced such accomplishments by his patron that lacked papal counterpart. The poet had offered his work to Reims and Rome, and where Manasses had endorsed him, papal support had not been forthcoming.[170] The implication is that the presentation of *De nuptiis* in Rome had been intended primarily to gain sponsorship for the poet and his work, rather than the patron and his cause.

Fulcoius' sour words about Rome bespeak a failure. The manuscript evidence does the same. *De nuptiis* survives in only three witnesses. They

Proceedings of the Third International Conference on Medieval Latin Studies (Cambridge, 9–12 September 1998), 2 vols. (Turnhout: Brepols, 2002), vol. I, pp. 144–57, and T. Haye, 'Christliche und pagane Dichtung bei Fulcoius von Beauvais', ibid., pp. 398–409, at 406–7.

[168] As for Fulcoius, *Ep.* 7 to Alexander II, ed. Colker, pp. 226–7, it opens with a short description of a journey to Rome, suggesting a date after the Roman presentation of *De nuptiis*. Colker's dating, 1069 × 1073, is rejected here as too cautious. The letters to Gregory and Hugh are Fulcoius, *Ep.* 2 and 3, ed. Colker, pp. 212–16; the former apparently refers to *De nuptiis*: 'Qui tibi leuitae scribsi, scribo tibi papae.'

[169] Fulcoius, *De nuptiis*, ed. Rousseau, i.11–12.

[170] Fulcoius, *Ep.* 26, ed. Colker, p. 268.

come from regions not far from his own sphere of activity, hinting that the primary transmission had been a local affair through his own networks. None the less, one impact is ascribable to his having taken *De nuptiis* to Rome. Sometime during the first half of the twelfth century, an anonymous epitaphist at Beauvais affirmed that 'Beauvais [and] Reims together with Rome desired' to hold Fulcoius after his death.[171] As regards Rome, such hyperbole must ultimately derive from Fulcoius' having commended *De nuptiis* to the pope; his other dealings with Rome were characterised conspicuously by Manasses' disaster.[172] What reasons explain the lack of papal enthusiasm is now only a matter for speculation. Fulcoius apparently did not have effective contacts in Rome who could have recommended him. Association with Manasses was a liability. Furthermore, like his patron, the poet was not a reformer in the mould of Alexander II and Hildebrand. While the imposition of clerical celibacy was among the most imperative of papal objectives, Fulcoius could conditionally defend clerical marriage and relish eros.[173] There was an ongoing controversy as to whether clerical marriage could be sanctioned or should be eradicated, with heated contributions in support of both positions.[174] From the Roman point of view, Fulcoius was on the wrong side.

4.2 A Textbook for Schools

Equipped with a prefatory verse address to the pope, *De nuptiis* chimes with Arator's *Historia apostolica*, regularly accompanied by his dedicatory address to the pope in manuscripts. Arator had served as a school-text for centuries and Latin teachers in Fulcoius' time would have noted the parallel. *De nuptiis* was, I would argue, targeted at schools, to be used as a textbook

---

[171] Fulcoius, *De nuptiis*, ed. Rousseau, 'Appendix II', p. 125: 'Beluacus, Remis cum Roma quem cupierunt, Meldis habet, seruat, fert, ueneratur et amat.'

[172] See n. 168 above.

[173] Fulcoius, *Epp.* 10, 16 and 19, ed. Colker, pp. 234–45, 251–2, 256–9; see T. C. Moser, Jr, *A Cosmos of Desire. The Medieval Latin Erotic Lyric in English Manuscripts* (Ann Arbor: The University of Michigan Press, 2004), pp. 23–9.

[174] E. van Houts, *Married Life in the Middle Ages, 900–1300* (Oxford University Press, 2019), pp. 170–91.

like the *Historia apostolica*. The evidence of reception offered by the manuscripts is critical here. Beauvais, BM, MS 11 is our richest witness to Fulcoius' extant writings, many of which survive nowhere else.[175] The volume, on palaeographical evidence, dates roughly from the first third of the twelfth century. Later provenance, and perhaps origin, is Beauvais cathedral: the earliest positive attestation to that effect is a library mark from the thirteenth century.[176] The inclusion of two papal letters to the bishop and clergy of Beauvais, copied in a contemporary hand, hints that the manuscript was perhaps made at the cathedral.[177] The volume conveys an anthology of Fulcoius' writings with some contemporary insertions. The text is written in a library hand of fine quality. By its physical dimensions, 25 × 17 cm, the volume has the appearance of a library book. Schoolbooks tended to be smaller, especially those in personal use.[178] However, institutionally produced books for the schoolroom could be considerably larger than the Beauvais book: Chartres, BM, MS 497, a near contemporary copy lost in the Second World War, was 52.5 × 36.5 cm and was produced under Thierry of Chartres († c.1150) for the school of Chartres.[179] As regards the Fulcoius manuscript, Beauvais MS 11, it has been proposed that lacunae in

---

[175] For the contents, see H. Omont, 'Épitaphes métriques en l'honneur de différents personnages du XIe siècle composées par Foulcoie de Beauvais, archidiacre de Meaux', *Mélanges Julien Havet* (Paris: E. Leroux, 1895), pp. 211–36, at 214–18. For codicology (without an analysis of the hands) and provenance, see Fulcoius, *De nuptiis*, ed. Rousseau, 'Introduction', pp. 56–64.

[176] For the evidence (library marks and booklists), see H. Omont, 'Recherches sur la bibliothèque de l'église cathédrale de Beauvais', *Mémoires de l'institut national de France*, 40 (1916), 1–93, at 51, 53; 'Épitaphes métriques', 213; and Fulcoius, *De nuptiis*, ed. Rousseau, 'Introduction', p. 57. For the dating, see Boutémy, 'Chronologie', 84.

[177] Fols. 76r–77r; Urban II, *Epistolae*, 103 and 104, *PL*, 151, cols. 283–552, at 378–40, to Bishop Fulk and the clergy and people of Beauvais respectively.

[178] For the dimensions of books in general, see R. Gameson, 'The material fabric of early British books', in R. Gameson (ed.), *The Cambridge History of the Book in Britain*, vol. 1 (Cambridge University Press, 2012), pp. 11–93, at 21–7.

[179] H. Omont, A. Molinier, C. Couderc and E. Coyecque, *Catalogue général des manuscrits des bibliothèques publiques de France. Départements. Tome XI: Chartres*

several verses and certain gross errors resulted from direct transmission from an untidy authorial working copy that was difficult to decipher.[180] The suggestion is fascinating but unverifiable. On the basis of the contents, early date and provenance, one may, however, speculate without very much trouble that the book was made or commissioned by an admirer who had known Fulcoius in person. The margins are almost entirely devoid of annotation, indicating that later consultation was infrequent at best. Importantly, a near contemporary hand inserted a short biography of Fulcoius on the recto of the final front flyleaf. The text, preserved in this manuscript and BnF, lat. 5305 (to be introduced shortly), is given below in English translation.

> Fulcoisus was born at Beauvais. He chose the Elysium of Meaux for study, where at the prompting of his teachers, especially Archbishop Manasses of Reims, he put together in a useful and seemly manner three volumes containing ten books in heroic metre. The first [comprises] one [book] of letters, epitaphs and some light-hearted stories, which he called *Vtrum* for the sake of experiment. The second [comprises] two [books], which he titled *Neutrum* because, exercising his skill in lives of certain great saints, he did not presume to advance so far as he wished and because this intermediate [volume] formed a continuum neither to the first volume nor to the last. Inspired by the Holy Spirit, he composed a third [volume] of seven books in the form of a dialogue between the Spirit and Man by means of a pious work [and] a marvellous poem, which he titled *Vtrumque on the Marriage of the Church*, for the reason that marrying the Old and New Testament, he betrothed a chaste virgin, namely the Church, to one man, Jesus Christ, Word of the

(Paris: Plon, 1890), 211–12. I thank Dr Jaakko Tahkokallio for pointing out this manuscript to me.

[180] Boutémy, 'Chronologie', 84–5.

Father, bringer of grace, who made both [Testaments]
one.[181]

The piece reads as an *accessus* to Fulcoius.[182] *Accessus* were standardised
introductions to equip readers with basic information about authors and
their works. There were several schemes by which to construct an *accessus*.
Our specimen echoes a pattern derivative of an introduction to Virgil's
Aeneid by Servius, a fourth-century grammarian. It accounted for the life of
the poet, title of the work, genre of the poem, intention of the writer,
number of books, order of books and explanation.[183] *Accessus* were composed predominantly on books and authors read in the classroom, most
notably poets, pagan and Christian. The party responsible for the insertion
of the *accessus* to Fulcoius in the Beauvais manuscript apparently understood that the volume was to serve the needs of students. Explained with
more verbose attention than given to the other works, *De nuptiis* was the
focus.

The hand who prefixed the *accessus* had not authored it. He was
a copyist, as is obvious from several errors from which our other copy is

---

[181] Fulcoius, *De nuptiis*, ed. Rousseau, 'Introduction', p. 16: 'Fulcoius genere
Beluacensis fuit. Meldis elisium studio elegit, ubi doctorum instinctu suorum
precipue archipresulis Manasse Remensis tria uolumina per decem libros utiliter
et decenter eroice composuit. Primum simplex in epistolis, in titulis, in
quibusdam quasi nugis, quod experientiae causa *Vtrum* nominauit. Secundum
uero duplex, quod *Neutrum* appellauit, eo quod in quorumdam uita sanctorum
ingenium exercens nec adhuc quod desiderabat agredi praesumens nec primo
uolumini nec ultimo medium continuauit. Tertium autem per vii libros
septiformi afflatus spiritu sub dialogo spiritus et hominis fideli opere, mirifico
carmine contexuit, quod *Vtrumque de nuptiis ecclesiae* titulauit hac de causa quod
uetus et nouum maritans testamentum Christo Iesu, Verbo Patris, latori gratiae,
qui fecit utraque unum, uni uiro uirginem castam, ecclesiam scilicet, despondit.'

[182] Ibid., p. 17; M. Manitius, *Geschichte der lateinischen Literatur des Mittelalters*, 3
vols. (Munich: Beck, 1911–31), vol. III, p. 837.

[183] *Accessus ad Auctores: Medieval Introductions to the Authors (Codex latinus
monacensis 19475)*, ed. S. M. Wheeler (Kalamazoo: Medieval Institute
Publications, 2015), 'Introduction', p. 2.

free.[184] That copy is the Paris manuscript, BnF, lat. 5305, a composite volume. The section relevant to us, folios 49–110, dates roughly from the mid-twelfth century.[185] It originally contained two treatises by Anselm, *De processione Spiritus sancti* and *Epistola de sacrificio azimi et fermentati*. Not very long after, Fulcoius' *De nuptiis* was appended on fols. 67v–110r and then, again soon after, the *accessus* was copied in an empty space on fol. 67r. Medieval provenance and perhaps origin is Fécamp, a Norman abbey, where the volume was attested in the fifteenth century and possibly as early as the twelfth.[186] Anselm's treatises were intended for the edification of mature brethren rather than Latin students. The volume's physical aspects are likewise appropriate to a library book: it is written in a book-hand of average quality and measures 27 × 19 cm.

The insertion of the *accessus* points toward the classroom, as do annotations by an early thirteenth-century reader, probably a monk of Fécamp. He entered notes in the margins of Fulcoius' poem but did not comment on Anselm's treatises. His entries were in the main brief captions such as 'On the governance of Jewish people as understood according to the moral interpretation from the first of the Kings etc.'[187] Upon engaging with the text more deeply, his guidance smacked more distinctly of school instruction. The annotation quoted below elucidates the conclusion of Book 1's prefatory section, introduces the work's two interlocutors, and alerts readers to indicators in the margins that identify which interlocutor is speaking.

> Here the author presents his book to the archbishop of
> Reims, announcing to him the two persons introduced in

---

[184] Variant readings, including obvious scribal errors, are reported in Fulcoius, *De nuptiis*, ed. Rousseau, 'Introduction', p. 16.

[185] Cf. R. Sharpe, 'Anselm as author: publishing in the late eleventh century', *Journal of Medieval Latin*, 19 (2009), 1–87, at 54.

[186] See a list of contents on fol. 110v, identified as coming from Fécamp. For the inconclusive twelfth-century evidence, see Fulcoius, *De nuptiis*, ed. Rousseau, 'Introduction', pp. 67–8 notes 243–4.

[187] Ibid., p. 52*: 'De regime gentis Iudaice ut moraliter intelligatur a primo regum et cetera.'

this work, calling one of those persons 'man', to whom he grants the task of inquiry, and the other 'spirit', to whom he gives the task of response. These two persons will be indicated in the outer margin when appropriate.[188]

Our last manuscript, BnF, lat. 16701, is a booklet, entirely dedicated to Fulcoius. The contents are as follows: epitaphs in his honour, his eulogy to Manasses, the above-mentioned verse address to Pope Alexander and Hildebrand, and then, from folio 4v to the end, *De nuptiis*.[189] The manuscript originated in an unknown centre in northern France in the latter half of the twelfth century. By its physical dimensions, 18 × 12 cm, it has the appearance of a book produced for the classroom or personal use. Marginalia accompany *De nuptiis*, but these are rather sparse.[190] Their precise relation to the text is often hard to establish, such that the perspective from which the work was approached cannot be determined with confidence. A later medieval *ex libris* on folio 91r associates the volume with teaching. It states that the manuscript came into the possession of the Sorbonne from Peter of Limoges – who authored an influential allegorical treatise on the eye, taught at the Sorbonne and bequeathed more than 120 volumes to it in 1306[191] – and that it was deposited 'inter grammaticalia', that is, among the textbooks used for Latin instruction. Accordingly, the manuscript, itemised as 'auctor de nupciis Christi et Ecclesie', appears among 'libri grammaticales' in a Sorbonne booklist of 1338.[192] That section of the library housed seventy volumes of works used in the teaching of Latin

---

[188] Ibid., p. 7*: 'Hic presentat actor librum suum Archiepiscopo Remensis, denuncians ei duas personas in hoc opus introductas, uocans unam personarum illarum hominem cui tribuit officium querendi, et aliam spiritum cui dat officium respondendi. Signabuntur itaque hec persone exterius in margine ut uidebitur expedire.'

[189] The description relies on ibid., pp. 64–6 and Plate 2.   [190] See Ibid., p. 56*.

[191] R. H. Rouse, 'The early library of the Sorbonne II', *Scriptorium*, 21 (1967), 227–51, at 227.

[192] A. Franklin, *Les anciennes bibliothèques de Paris*, 3 vols. (Paris: Imprimerie Impériale, 1867–74), vol. I, p. 309.

at various levels. Pagan authors, such as Ovid, Virgil, Sallust, Statius and others, often found in multiple copies, prevailed. Among the grammarians were of course Priscian and Donatus, and there were many vocabularies. The only biblical epic itemised in the list is Fulcoius's *De nuptiis*.

It would be naive to propose on the basis of a single booklist that Fulcoius had replaced Arator and late-antique biblical epicists at the Sorbonne. Rather, the vagaries of transmission – in this case, belonging to a bequest – explain the case. While we cannot know whether or not *De nuptiis* was ever used as a school-text at the Sorbonne, the document helpfully demonstrates that it was categorised as such there. The booklist also captures something of Fulcoius' ambition. He sought to be counted among the great Christian epicists read in the classroom. Such aspirations are evident in his efforts to associate *De nuptiis* with their works by a denunciation of pagan literature. The introductory section to Book 1 disapproves of the classics as 'puerile'.[193] Pagan gods and works are denied entry to the poem, because 'it is shameful to admit pigs to a beautiful meadow'.[194] The motif of favouring biblical and Christian authors over pagan ones is reiterated multiple times in the sections that follow.[195] Such affirmations were a rhetorical affectation. Fulcoius' poetic art was imbued with classical reading, avidly cited in his other works. Even *De nuptiis* occasionally adduces pagan concepts without an air of criticism. An instance is a description of Fulcoius' own education in the seven liberal arts. These, he explains, emanated from Pallas Athena.[196] That allegorical notion points towards Martianus Capella's *De nuptiis Philologiae et Mercurii*, commonly read in schools at the time. It might be added that the title of Fulcoius' poem was certainly a deliberate allusion to that work.[197] The renunciation of pagan learning was a motif in Christian Latin poetry. Juvencus and Sedulius, for instance, condemned pagan poetry in the prefaces to their

---

[193] Fulcoius, *De nuptiis*, ed. Rousseau, i.13.

[194] Ibid., i.25–6: 'Heu pudet in stellis lumen fuscasse procellis / floribus et grato porcos ammittere prato.'

[195] Ibid., v.297–9, vi.206–18, vii.1295–6. [196] Ibid., v.334–62.

[197] Ibid., 'Introduction', pp. 43–4.

Gospel versifications.[198] By doing the same, Fulcoius complied with an established textbook convention.[199]

De nuptiis did not achieve any great impact. Three surviving manuscripts and one probable allusion about fifty years later, in the *Hypognosticon* of Lawrence of Durham, is a bleak tally for an author who had sought the favour of the pope and emperor.[200] The sparseness of the transmission probably had more to do with the milieu of Fulcoius' career than his literary craft. At the time, new biblical epics were rare. Only two such attempts beside *De nuptiis* are known from the eleventh century, neither of which attracted notable attention.[201] It has been observed recently that relative to pagan classics, the late-antique Christian epicists who had dominated the Latin classroom for centuries, Arator among them, gradually lost ground from the eleventh century onwards.[202] The trend was perhaps a factor in undermining the potential of *De nuptiis* to find readers who taught at schools. However, had Fulcoius lived two or three generations later, his epic would have had better prospects. Grand biblical versifications re-emerged as a fashionable genre for original composition in the twelfth century. Several new works were written, of which some obtained

---

[198] Juvencus, *Euangeliorum libri IV*, Prologus, ed. J. Huemer, *CSEL*, 24 (1891), pp. 1–2; Sedulius, *Carmen paschale*, i.17–28, ed. J. Huemer, *CSEL*, 10 (1885), pp. 16–17.

[199] For a more comprehensive analysis, see Haye, 'Christliche und pagane Dichtung', pp. 399–406.

[200] Fulcoius, *De nuptiis*, ed. Rousseau, 'Introduction', p. 47.

[201] G. Dinkova-Bruun, 'Biblical versifications from late antiquity to the middle of the thirteenth century: history or allegory?', in W. Otten and K. Pollman (eds.), *Poetry and Exegesis in Premodern Latin Christianity. The Encounter between Classical and Christian Strategies of Interpretation* (Leiden: Brill, 2007), pp. 315–42, at 325–6. The versifications in question, Henry of Augsburg's *Planctus Evae* and the anonymous *De conditione mundi*, survive in two manuscripts and in a single fragment respectively.

[202] J. Tahkokallio, 'The classicization of the Latin curriculum and "the Renaissance of the Twelfth Century": a quantitative study of the codicological evidence', *Viator*, 46 (2015), 129–54, at 132–4 and passim.

considerable readerships.[203] Lawrence's *Hypognosticon*, which survives in at least twenty-three manuscripts, including many from the twelfth century, is a case in point.[204]

An unusual new composition at the time, *De nuptiis* would have needed effective promotion to be a success. Fulcoius had the wrong patron. Affiliation to Manasses, which *De nuptiis* exhibits in a conspicuous fashion, is likely to have proved counterproductive in the pursuit of readers outside his sphere of direct influence. It did not help that Manasses' worst nemesis was Hugh of Die, papal legate.[205] Advocates of the papal cause would hardly be persuaded by the archbishop's endorsement. A preface reporting that the author had gifted the pope a copy in person was not enough. Active papal contribution to publication, not received, could have made a difference. As is shown in the next chapter, Hugh of Die's endorsement of Anselm's *Monologion* and *Proslogion* in his capacity as papal legate is a demonstration of how valuable such support could be.

---

[203] Dinkova-Bruun, 'Biblical versifications', 328–32.
[204] R. Sharpe, *A Handlist of the Latin Writers of Great Britain and Ireland before 1540* (Turnhout: Brepols, 1997; supplement with additions and corrections, 2001), pp. 431–2.
[205] See p. 41 above.

5 Anselm, Hugh of Die and Pope Urban II

Anselm, prior and abbot of Bec (1063–93) and archbishop of Canterbury (1093–1109), explored Christian faith by way of discursive reasoning. While other teachers did the same, the programmatic nature of his method was a radical departure, in that it mostly eschewed the citation of authorities, of which the Bible and Church Fathers were the most central. As a result, Anselm met with censure at the beginning of his literary career. He overcame his detractors, however, and came to be regarded as a preeminent theological voice, whose works were read across Latin Christendom.[206] This chapter argues that a significant factor in his rise to intellectual eminence was his connexion with the papacy. Jerome's association with Pope Damasus is used as a hermeneutical key.

5.1 The Monologion *and* Proslogion: *Hugh of Die, Papal Legate to France*

Anselm began his authorial career in the Norman monastery of Bec, where he served as prior from 1063 to 1078 and then as abbot until he was elevated to the archbishopric of Canterbury in 1093. He completed his first treatise, the *Monologion*, a sustained contemplation on some key aspects of God's essence, in 1077 or one or two years before that. He consigned it for inspection to Archbishop Lanfranc of Canterbury, his former teacher at Bec. The archbishop disapproved of the method by which conclusions were drawn by argument from reason without the citation of authoritative texts

---

[206] While Anselm's literary career has often been regarded as a stroll from strength to strength, three recent papers show that his own efforts towards dissemination were crucial. Sharpe, 'Anselm as author' scrutinises his determination to obtain readerships; G. Gasper, 'Envy, jealousy, and the boundaries of orthodoxy: Anselm of Canterbury and the genesis of the *Proslogion*', *Viator*, 41 (2010), 45–68, and S. Niskanen, 'Anselm's predicament: the *Proslogion* and anti-intellectual rhetoric in the aftermath of the Berengarian Controversy', *Journal of the History of Ideas*, 82 (2021), 547–68 demonstrate and assess the initial resistance he encountered among his brethren, a starting point for the discussion here.

as evidence.[207] Other readers, too, were baffled and further criticism flowed. This demonstrably undermined Anselm's confidence. In 1077 or 1078 Abbot Rainald, perhaps of Saint-Cyprien at Poitiers, asked for a copy of the *Monologion*. In his response, Anselm explained his situation as follows.

> I should never consign to you the little work you assiduously requested from afar, were I able to disobey your will. For I fear that when it comes into the hands of persons who are more keen to criticise than seek to understand what they hear, and if they might perhaps read something therein that they have neither heard nor thought of before, they at once cry that I have written something that is unheard of and contrary to the truth. But because, as I live far away, I could say nothing in answer in such a case, they would not only consider themselves promotors of the truth while actually rejecting it, but also rashly persuade other credulous men that I champion error, even before they hear what it is that they rebuke. I have already suffered by the too-rushed judgements of such men for what I, following Blessed Augustine, said about the persons and substance of God. . . . For this reason I strongly urge your holiness that you show that little work not to men who are garrulous and quarrelsome, but who are rational and peaceful.[208]

[207] Anselm, *Ep*. i.68.3–4, ed. S. Niskanen, *Letters of Anselm, Archbishop of Canterbury, I: The Bec Letters* (Oxford University Press, 2019), pp. 198–201.

[208] Ibid., i.74.2–3, pp. 214–17: 'Opusculum illud quod a me tanto studio de tam longe petitis nequaquam uobis mitterem, si uestrae uoluntati non oboedire potuissem. Timeo enim ne cum uenerit in manus aliquorum qui magis sunt intenti reprehendere quod audiunt quam intelligere, si forte ibi legerint aliquid quod anteac non audierunt necd animaduerterunt, statim clament me inaudita et ueritati repugnantia scripsisse. Quibus cum longe positus respondere non potero, non solum ipsi ueritatem negando ueritati se fauere opinabuntur, sed et aliis temere, antequam audiant quid sit quod ipsi reprehendant, credentibus me falsitatis assertorem persuadebunt. Iam enim talium passus sum nimis acceleratam reprehensionem ex eo quod secutus beatum Augustinum dixi de personis et de substantia Dei. . . . Quapropter uestram uehementer efflagito

Anselm composed his next treatise soon after, in 1077. This is the *Proslogion*, an ingenious fusion of prayer and ratiocination, renowned for the so-called ontological argument, a chain of reasoning which affirms the existence of God as a logical necessity. A milestone in Christian learning, the work is a *locus classicus* in modern scholarship. The beginnings were not promising, however. Detesting their prior's inquiries, a party within Anselm's own brethren at Bec sought to terminate the process of composition by stealing his draft. Anselm recomposed the lost text, but this new draft, on wax tablets, was soon found smashed. A third draft was made on parchment, which was harder to break and easier to conceal than tablets.[209] The assault should be considered an expression of severe disapproval.[210]

By his own admission, Anselm at first preferred not to prefix his own name to the *Monologion* and *Proslogion*. He circulated them only anonymously until in 1083 × 1085, Hugh of Die, archbishop of Lyon and papal legate to France, commanded that he sign them, that is, publish them under his own name. This unusual detail is known from a preface which Anselm inserted in the *Proslogion* upon complying with Hugh's command. The pertinent passage concludes the preface, a placement that can be taken as emphatic:

> But when both works had already been copied under these headings by a number of people, many of them forced me – above all the reverend Archbishop of Lyon, Hugh by name, who in his capacity as papal legate to Gaul commanded me thereof by apostolic authority – to write my name at their top. So that this could be done more conveniently, I named one *Monologion*, that is an internal discussion, and the other *Proslogion*, that is a conversation addressed to someone.[211]

sanctitatem ut idem opusculum non uerbosis et litigiosis hominibus sed rationabilibus et quietis ostendat.'

[209] Eadmer, *Vita S. Anselmi*, i.19, ed. R. W. Southern (Oxford University Press, 1972), pp. 30–1.

[210] Gasper, 'Envy, jealousy', 46–7, 61, 68; Niskanen, 'Anselm's predicament', 550–1, 561.

[211] Anselm, *Proslogion*, Prooemium, *SAO*, 1, p. 94: 'Sed cum iam a pluribus cum bis titulis utrumque transcriptum esset, coegerunt me plures et maxime reuerendus

Much in the preface to the *Proslogion* is cliché, but the quoted account of Hugh's legatine action must have been accurate in its detail, not least for the reason that the legate himself received a copy of the work.[212] A distorted testimony would have been an offence. The two treatises, which had previously been transmitted singly, were now paired together. They became twins. That relationship was communicated through the stressed analogy between their new titles. Previously, they had been called *Exemplum meditandi de ratione fidei* and *Fides quaerens intellectum*, which Anselm revised as *Monologion* and *Proslogion* respectively.[213]

The pairing of the works, which involved the retitling, the authorial signature and the insertion of the preface in the *Proslogion*, constituted veritable republication. Stressing the provisional aspect of his texts' former circulation, Anselm represented this event as the first publication proper. The crux of the whole affair was that he ascribed the republication to a command from Hugh of Die. He 'above all' had urged Anselm to sign the *Monologion* and *Proslogion*. The detail that Hugh had acted in his capacity as papal legate was plainly of moment to Anselm. For he cared to remark on it twice within a single sentence: 'fungens ... legatione apostolica ... apostolica praecepit auctoritate'. These were not empty words. From the second half of the eleventh century onwards, the legatine dignity was a principal instrument by which the papacy took effective action and implemented reformist policies across Latin Christendom. On the word of *Dictatus papae*, a concept for a canonical collection designed by or under the oversight of Pope Gregory VII, 'his legate, even if of lower rank, precedes all bishops in a council and can impose the sentence of deposition on them'.[214] Hugh, who was prepared to depose the archbishop of Reims, as

---

archiepiscopus Lugdunensis, Hugo nomine, fungens in Gallia legatione apostolica, qui mihi hoc ex apostolica praecepit auctoritate, ut nomen meum illis praescriberem. Quod ut aptius fieret, illud quidem *Monologion*, id est soliloquium, istud uero *Proslogion*, id est alloquium, nominaui.'

212 Anselm, *Ep.* i.88.3, ed. Niskanen, p. 258.

213 Ibid., i.94.2, p. 274, and n. 211 above.

214 Gregory VII, *Registrum*, ii.55a, ed. Caspar, p. 203: 'Quod legatus eius omnibus episcopis presit in concilio etiam inferioris gradus et adversus eos sententiam

shown in the previous chapter, understood his legatine status in those terms.[215]

Hugh's mandate to Anselm was a serious matter, but it has never been assessed in the wider context of Roman legatine action. What follows is a brief survey of how papal legates engaged in authorial publication in roles other than that of author. Cases up to *c*.1150 were harvested digitally from *A Database for Medieval Publication Networks*, a work in progress, which embraces most of the identifiable Latin works from Britain and Ireland before *c*.1540, and manually from the *Patrologia Latina*, the result of reading all medieval prefatory texts. The corpus is not exhaustive, but, comprising items in the thousands, it is sufficiently large for the needs of this review. Seven cases emerged, summarised below. The principal observation is that our other writers did not see fit to underline the legatine office and authority to the extent Anselm did in the prologue to the *Proslogion*.

In 1094 Bernold of Constance, monk of Schaffhausen, who was an intellectual protagonist in the German investiture contest, received a commission to compose an exposition on the status of ordinations and baptisms administered by excommunicates.[216] This came from Bishop Gebhard III of Constance, papal legate. A short collage of authoritative extracts, the piece has been regarded as 'a position paper' for Gebhard, who needed it for the papal council of Piacenza, to convene the following year.[217] Nothing suggests that a wider audience was being sought, and as such the exposition cannot be considered a publication in the same sense as Anselm's treatises. Gebhard and Bernold had also collaborated previously, and the exposition should be considered one fruit

---

depositionis possit dare.' For Gregory's intentions, see H. E. J. Cowdrey, *Gregory VII 1073–1085* (Oxford: Clarendon Press, 1998), pp. 503, 595.

[215] For a broader discussion, see Rennie, *Legatine Work of Hugh of Die*, esp. pp. 64–73.

[216] Bernold of Constance, *De reordinatione vitanda et de salute parvulorum qui ab excommunicatis baptizati sunt*, ed. F. Thaner, MGH, *Libelli de lite*, 2 (Hanover: Hahn, 1892), pp. 150–6.

[217] R. Somerville, *Pope Urban II's Council of Piacenza* (Oxford University Press, 2011), p. 24. *PL*, 148, cols. 1255–66.

of a longer working relationship between a scholar and his diocesan. In 1115 or 1116, Alexander, monk of Canterbury, put together a collection of Anselm's memorable sayings. The work was a commission from Abbot Anselm of San Saba at Rome, papal legate to England. The connexion between the author and commissioner had nothing to do with the legateship, however; it flowed from their relationship with the protagonist. Alexander had been one of the most trusted servants of the late Archbishop Anselm, who happened to be the legate's uncle.[218] In about 1133, Arnulf, archdeacon of Sées, later bishop of Lisieux, wrote an invective against Bishop Girard of Angoulême to denounce his support for 'antipope' Anacletus. He sent the work to Bishop Geoffrey of Chartres, the reasons for which were practical and political. Geoffrey had been Arnulf's patron, and, in his capacity as papal legate to Aquitaine, the man was Anacletus' main opponent in France.[219] Next, Brother Geoffrey of Tiron wrote a life of Bernard, the founder of his house, in 1137 × 1143.[220] The work was dedicated to the same Bishop Geoffrey of Chartres who had requested it to be written.[221] Geoffrey was the diocesan of Tiron and its benefactor. That local connexion, rather than Geoffrey's legatine dignity, accounts for the dedication. The same applies to our next case, a short liturgical treatise from 1137 × 1152. The author, Brother John of Echternach, an obscure figure otherwise unknown, dedicated it to Archbishop Adalbero of Trier, papal legate. As John did not emphasise Adalbero's legatine dignity, we must assume that his dedication belongs to the fact that Adalbero was John's diocesan.[222] In 1138 or 1139, Osbert of

---

[218] Alexander of Canterbury, *Liber de dictis beati Anselmi*, Prologus, in *Memorials of St Anselm*, ed. R. W. Southern and F. S. Schmitt (Oxford University Press, 1969), pp. 105–270, at 107.

[219] Arnulf of Lisieux, *Invectiva in Girardum*, ed. J. Dieterich, MGH, *Libelli de lite*, 3 (Hanover: Hahn, 1897), pp. 85–107, at 86.

[220] See K. Thompson, *The Monks of Tiron: A Monastic Community and Religious Reform in the Twelfth Century* (Cambridge University Press, 2014), pp. 53, 136.

[221] Geoffroy of Tiron, *Vita beati Bernardi*, PL, 172, cols. 1363–446, at 1370.

[222] John of Echternach, *De tribus missis in nativitate Domini celebrandis*, PL, 166, cols. 1509–14.

Clare consigned a copy of *Vita beati Edwardi* to Cardinal-Bishop Alberic of Ostia, papal legate. Part of the project to secure a papal canonisation for King Edward the Confessor, the letter requested Alberic's help in the process.[223] In 1145, upon their joint preaching mission to the heretics of Nantes, the same Cardinal-Bishop Alberic of Ostia, papal legate to southern France, requested that Hugh of Amiens, archbishop of Rouen, compose a treatise on the subject. Hugh completed the work somewhat later than expected, but he considered it a commission from Alberic, to whom he consigned it. The salutation addresses Alberic with his apostolic designations. His status as a papal delegate is not referred to elsewhere.[224]

This survey shows papal legates to have been commissioners and dedicatees, normal protagonists in medieval publishing. In three cases the bond ensued from the legate's status as diocesan of the author in question rather than from his apostolic legateship. Such affairs do not embody any deliberate attempts to draw Rome into authorial domains. Rather, they attest to the expansion of the papal apparatus by employing bishops outside Italy as legates. The dedicatees of the remaining four texts were not the authors' diocesans. In these cases, the dedicatees' legatine mission was not the relevant factor, but rather their potential to advance a canonisation in Rome or the fact of a family relationship. None of these aspects pertains to Anselm's connexion with Hugh of Die. He was not Anselm's diocesan, and there is no evidence of any previous association between them, let alone collaboration. Hugh acted neither as Anselm's dedicatee nor, at least in the conventional sense, the commissioner.

Hugh's intervention was unparalleled as a legatine act. Yet, in its essence it echoed an age-old, but mostly inoperative, notion that Rome could reject and commend writings. This was expressed in a fully developed form with regard to works already published in a spurious decretal known as *De libris recipiendis et non recipiendis*, purportedly issued by Pope Gelasius (†496).

---

[223] Osbert of Clare, *Ep.* 14, ed. E. W. Williamson, *Letters of Osbert of Clare, Prior of Westminster* (Oxford University Press, 1929), pp. 80–3.

[224] Hugh of Amiens, *Contra haereticos sui temporis sive de ecclesia et eius ministris libri tres*, *PL*, 192, cols. 1255–98, at 1255–6. R. B. Freeburn, *Hugh of Amiens and the Twelfth-Century Renaissaince* (Farnham: Ashgate, 2011), 147–8.

Datable to the sixth century, the document is the earliest extant list of books commended and prohibited by the papacy.[225] The document enjoyed a very wide circulation since it was incorporated in the ubiquitous Pseudo-Isidorian decretals in the Carolingian period.[226] It also found its way into several other collections such as the so-called *Collectio Lanfranci*, which Anselm demonstrably perused at Bec.[227] Pope Nicholas I (†867) explicitly entertained the idea that the papacy could also censor new writings at will. Two of his letters may be instanced here. One, addressed to Emperor Charles the Bald, advised that the recent translation by John Scottus Eriugena of *De diuinis nominibus* of the pseudo-Dionysius the Areopagite should have been sent to the pope 'to be approved or rejected by our judgement according to custom'. Nicholas asked that the work be immediately despatched so that 'once it is approved by our apostolic judgment, it may instantly be more favourably regarded by all on account of our authority'.[228] The letter seems to have faded into oblivion until it resurfaced in the canonical collection of Cardinal Atto of San Marco, put together in Rome apparently in the 1070s. Its next known application is in an unknown manuscript bearing a text similar to the one found in Paris, Bibliothèque de l'Arsenal, MS 713, fol. 139r–v. Using that lost manuscript as his source, Ivo of Chartres (†1115) included the letter in his *Decretum*.[229] Ivo was an

---

[225] *Decretum Gelasianum de libris recipiendis et non recipiendis*, ed. E. von Dobschütz (Leipzig: Hinrichs, 1912), pp. 340–52.

[226] *Decretales pseudo-Isidorianae et capitula Angilramni*, ed. P. Hinschius (Leipzig: Tauchnitz, 1863), pp. 635–7.

[227] Cambridge, Trinity College, MS B. 16. 44, pp. 161–3; Anselm, *Ep.* i.56.6, ed. Niskanen, p. 166, n. 11.

[228] Nicholas I, *Ep.* 130, ed. E. Perels, MGH, *Epistolae*, 6 (Berlin: Weidmann, 1925), pp. 257–690, at 651: 'Quod iuxta morem nobis mitti et nostro debuit iudicio approbari uel reprobari . . . nobis praefatum opus sine ulla cunctatione mittat, quatinus, dum a nostri apostolatus iudicio fuerit approbatum, ab omnibus incunctanter nostra auctoritate acceptius habeatur.'

[229] R. Somerville, 'Pope Nicholas I and John Scottus Eriugena: JE 2833', *Zeitschrift der Savigny-Stiftung für Rechtsgeschichte: Kanonistische Abteilung*, 83 (1997), 67–85, at 70–9.

acquaintance both of Anselm's and Hugh's.[230] The other pertinent letter by Nicholas I was sent to the bishops in Gaul. In it he asserted that the pope had authority to approve or reject writings.[231] The letter was frequently copied, from the Carolingian period onwards. At some point it was incorporated in books containing the Pseudo-Isidorian Decretals in France and Normandy.[232] Ivo of Chartres included it in his *Tripartita* and *Decretum*. They greatly abbreviate the letter, which is lengthy, so that the statement on papal prerogative to commend or dismiss written works comes first.[233] The text in the *Tripartita* consists only of the clause on the papal prerogative to censor writings, evidencing Ivo's focus on the subject.

No claim is made here that Hugh or Anselm would have read or known Nicholas' letters. Rather, the letters' transmission suggests that in their circles it was accepted that the pope, and by implication his legates, were possessed of the privilege of sanctioning writings. Previously very uncommon, the application of such ideas embodied the reform papacy's activism and predisposition to intervene in local affairs. Another relevant manifestation of those reformist tendencies was the increasing attention Rome was paying to debate on doctrinal issues. This unavoidably led to its intervening in authorial book-circulation.

At this juncture, Jerome's collaboration with Pope Damasus in the production of a new Latin translation of the Gospels may be recalled. Part of their project was to prepare for the denunciation of Jerome's methodological preference for the Greek original over Latin tradition. Censure was expressed even as Jerome was still working. Such tensions

---

[230] For Anselm, see C. Rolker, *Canon Law and the Letters of Ivo of Chartres* (Cambridge University Press, 2010), pp. 7, 90–1; for Hugh, see Rennie, *Legatine Work of Hugh of Die*, pp. 42–3, 78–9, 207.

[231] Nicholas I, *Ep.* 71, ed. Perels, p. 394.

[232] A near-contemporary copy is BnF, lat. 5095, fol. 106r onwards while lat. 3854 fols. 212v–217v represents twelfth-century transmission in Normandy, perhaps at Jumièges.

[233] Ivo, *Decretum*, v.33 and *Collectio tripartita*, 1.62.10, https://ivo-of-chartres.github.io/decretum.html and https://ivo-of-chartres.github.io/tripartita/trip_a_1.pdf respectively, accessed 4 May 2021.

evoke Anselm's situation. The methodological approach of the *Monologion* had been explicitly disapproved of before publication; a party at Bec sought to terminate the composition of his next treatise, the *Proslogion*, by destroying and stealing its drafts. Hugh's extraordinary legatine command must belong to this context of reception. Hugh was certainly aware of strains surrounding dialectical discussions on divine mysteries. He had, for instance, participated in dealings leading to the condemnation of Berengar, a theologian who, among other things, was alleged to have preferred reason to faith.[234] So that the function of Hugh's command to Anselm can be appreciated in a general sense, Nicholas I's letter to Charles the Bald may be requoted: 'once approved by our apostolic judgement, [a writing] may instantly be more favourably regarded by all on account of our authority'.[235] By implication, Hugh's command was an apostolic certificate of the validity of Anselm's treatises.

Hugh's motive to intervene would have been connected to the bond between Bec and the reform papacy, which had been tied already in the 1050s, when Lanfranc, Anselm's predecessor as prior, lived there.[236] An indication of a special relationship exists in a letter from Pope Gregory VII to Anselm, which states that report of his 'good deeds' had reached the curia. The letter can only be dated as 1079 × 1085 and it cannot be known whether or not it was Hugh who had recommended Anselm to the pope.[237] It might be thought that an intellectual incentive would also have been a prerequisite for Hugh's action. He was an erudite reader, or so the books he bequeathed to his church would suggest. A list in a Lyon necrology betrays a fine personal library focused heavily on patristic theology, chief among which are the writings of St Augustine, with more than twenty individual titles attributed to him. Augustine was also Anselm's main

---

[234] H. E. J. Cowdrey, 'The Papacy and the Berengarian Controversy', in P. Ganz, R. Huygens and F. Niewöhner (eds.), *Auctoritas und Ratio: Studien zu Berengar von Tours* (Wiesbaden: Otto Harrassowitz, 1990), pp. 109–38, at 125.

[235] See n. 228 above.

[236] H. E. J. Cowdrey, *Lanfranc: Scholar, Monk, and Archbishop* (Oxford University Press, 2003), pp. 22–3.

[237] Anselm, *Ep.* i.108.2., ed. Niskanen, p. 318: 'fructuum tuorum'.

intellectual hero. A volume dedicated to the works of Boethius, whose rationalistic method of theological inquiry was much like Anselm's, is likewise included. Hugh also owned almost all of Anselm's treatises, but none of his prayers.[238] In his opinion, the man was an eminent teacher. When Anselm, then archbishop of Canterbury, was in exile 1097–1100, they became great friends. In demonstration of his admiration, Hugh always insisted on calling Anselm his 'master'.[239]

The literary *topos* of affected modesty, absolutely universal in medieval writing, can only have been of secondary importance for Hugh to have interfered and for Anselm to have published anonymously at first. Authorial anonymity belonged to expressions of modesty; and articulations of will-ingness to publish and disseminate anonymously but failure to do so – that is, that the author signed his work claiming that he would prefer not to – were a variant of it.[240] It seems very unlikely that Hugh's intention was simply to force Anselm to abandon any false modesty. Anonymous pub-lication in conformity with a literary *topos* would hardly have been an issue for someone who was not then among the author's associates. It is still more unlikely that compliance with convention would have prompted extraor-dinary legatine action, years after the first release. This is not to say that the modesty motif would not have been an incentive for Anselm to divulge the fact that he forsook anonymity because a papal legate had told him to. We know that he had more pressing concerns, however, and these must principally explain his repeated insistence that he published under an apostolic mandate. A statement from about 1140 supports this reading; Peter of Poitiers, secretary to the abbot of Cluny, proposed that some

---

[238] *Obituarium Lugdunensis ecclesiae: Nécrologe des personnages illustres et des bienfaiteurs de l'église métropolitaine de Lyon du IXe au XVe siècle*, ed. M.-C. Guigue (Lyon: Scheuring, 1867), pp. 129–30. Anselm had promised to gift Hugh his works; Anselm, *Ep.* i.94.2, ed. Niskanen, p. 274.

[239] Alexander of Canterbury, *De dictis Anselmi*, xlii, ed. Southern and Schmitt, p. 240.

[240] J. Schwietering, *Die Demutsformel mittelhochdeutscher Dichter* (Berlin: Weidmann, 1921), pp. 25–8.

contemporary writers suppressed their names for fear of accusations of falsity and heresy.[241]

How far Hugh's intervention silenced criticisms against the *Monologion* and *Proslogion* cannot be known, but it was certainly a powerful deterrent. His apostolic charges would have overruled the mandate of even the greatest local powers, including the authority of bishops and synods. It is of interest here that Archbishop Lanfranc, who, as noted above, had initially frowned upon the *Monologion*, soon afterwards came to endorse it. A dedicatory letter to him which Anselm prefixed to his work is implicit proof that he had a change of heart.[242] As archbishop of Canterbury, Lanfranc was a major source of ecclesiastical authority in the Anglo-Norman realm. But he was not Anselm's diocesan, and the impression is that his endorsement was considered less potent than Hugh's, received years later. For, as far as the evidence permits us to conclude, it was only after Hugh's legatine command that Anselm found the confidence to circulate the treatises without constraint.[243] Within a few years of the event, certainly before his translation to Canterbury in 1093, he recommended the *Proslogion* to a potential reader with assurance.[244] His reluctance to circulate the work was gone. In the early 1090s at the latest, he appended to the *Proslogion* a critique by Brother Gaunilo of Marmoutier of the ontological argument and his own reply to it.[245] Both sides of the dialogue operated from reason alone, and Anselm was unashamedly convinced of his method and conclusions.

5.2 De incarnatione Verbi *and* Commendatio operis*: Pope Urban II*

At the turn of the 1080s, Anselm, then abbot of Bec, became involved in a dispute on the nature of the Trinity.[246] The bone of contention was a new

[241] Peter of Poitiers, *Ep. ad Petrum abbatem Cluniacensem*, PL, 189, col. 47.

[242] Niskanen, 'Anselm's predicament', 550.　[243] Sharpe, 'Anselm as author', 17.

[244] Anselm, *Ep.* i.99.7, ed. Niskanen, p. 290.　[245] Sharpe, 'Anselm as author', 35.

[246] For a detailed discussion, see C. J. Mews, 'St Anselm, Roscelin and the See of Beauvais', in D. E. Luscombe and G. R. Evans (eds.), *Anselm: Aosta, Bec and Canterbury: Papers in Commemoration of the Nine-Hundredth Anniversary of*

Trinitarian proposition by Roscelin of Compiègne, a secular teacher, which was subsequently rejected as tritheism. Having been informed of Roscelin's proposition, Anselm sought to define his terminology in brief.[247] Soon afterwards he decided to compose a full-scale exposition in order to dissociate himself from the teachings of Roscelin, who had claimed that he and Anselm were essentially in agreement. On learning that a clerical assembly at Soissons had condemned Roscelin, Anselm considered the matter solved and halted his writing.[248] However, when visiting England in 1092–3, he was told that Roscelin was once again propagating his doctrine. He decided to resume the writing of his response.[249] Another delay, of an unknown length, followed after his appointment as archbishop of Canterbury on 6 March 1093. It is not clear precisely when the work met completion, but a short report by Eadmer, his assistant and biographer, implies that this was years rather than months before the Council of Bari in 1098.[250] Anselm titled the piece *Epistola de incarnatione Verbi* and dedicated it to Pope Urban II.

De incarnatione proved relevant to the said Council of Bari in southern Italy. The council was presided over by Urban II, being convened on 1 or 3 October 1098 and in session for a week. Exiled from England between 1097 and 1100, Anselm attended in person. He had met the pope on multiple occasions in the months before. Given the prominent role the pope

Anselm's Enthronement as Archbishop, 25 September 1093 (Sheffield Academic Press, 1996), pp. 106–19 and 'St Anselm and Roscelin: some new texts and their implications. I. The *De incarnatione Verbi* and the *Disputatio inter christianum et gentilem*', *Archives d'histoire doctrinale et littéraire du Moyen Âge*, 58 (1991), 55–98, at 57–67.

[247] Anselm, *Epp.* i.112 and i.143, ed. Niskanen, pp. 332–5, 406–9.

[248] Anselm, *Ep. de incarnatione Verbi*, 1, *SAO*, 2, p. 4.

[249] Anselm, *Ep.* i.128.2, ed. Niskanen, p. 376.

[250] Eadmer, *Vita Anselmi*, ii.10, ed. Southern, pp. 72–3. Mews, 'Anselm and Roscelin', 58, suggests that completion took place 'soon after' the appointment; Sharpe, 'Anselm as author', 22, 36–40, 42, 86, proposes the time-frame of 1093–4; R. W. Southern, *St Anselm. A Portrait in a Landscape* (Cambridge University Press, 1990), pp. xxvii and 180 suggests, respectively, the year 1094 and a point of time within two years of Anselm's election as archbishop.

conferred on him at the council, preparations must have been laid during their consultations. One of the chief issues to be discussed in the council was the integration of the Greek churches of southern Italy into the Roman obedience. A major obstacle was that great controversy between Latin and Greek Christianity on the *filioque* addition to the Nicene Creed. In Anselm, the pope had a champion who could lucidly propound the Catholic dogma of the Trinity, the doctrinal framework of the contest. Pope Urban assigned Anselm to deliver a plenary speech on the subject at Bari. It proved a great success, or at least the Latin delegates were much impressed. Underscoring Anselm's conciliar triumph, the pope quoted the *De incarnatione* in his response to the Greek party.[251] Papal citation had an impact on Anselm's audiences, as will be demonstrated in an essay on the subject that I have forthcoming.[252]

What concerns us here is that, at one of their meetings in 1098, Anselm presented a copy of his work to Urban II, to which he had prefixed a dedicatory note, titled *Commendatio operis ad Vrbanum papam II* in its most recent edition, henceforth *Commendatio*. The presentation copy does not survive, and manuscripts of Anselm's treatises representative of primary circulation do not transmit that piece.[253] The implication from the latter is that *Commendatio* was intended exclusively for the volume gifted to the pope. Yet, attested by at least twenty-two manuscripts, it gained a relatively wide circulation. While *Commendatio* identifies its mother text only as 'subditum opusculum' ('the work appended'), our manuscripts attach it either to *De incarnatione* or *Cur Deus homo*, Anselm's largest treatise, which he finished in Italy some weeks before the Council of Bari.[254] Printed editions previous to the first critical edition, by F. S. Schmitt, affix

[251] Somerville, *Council of Piacenza*, pp. 125–7; Eadmer, *Vita Anselmi*, ii.29, 33–34, ed. Southern, pp. 104–6, 110–13; Eadmer, *Historia nouorum in Anglia*, ed. M. Rule, Rolls Series (London: Longman, 1884), pp. 95–106.

[252] S. Niskanen, 'From author to authority: Anselm's public reputation and the Council of Bari (1098)', *Journal of Medieval History* (forthcoming).

[253] For a list, see Sharpe, 'Anselm as author', 80–7.

[254] Eadmer, *Vita Anselmi*, ii.30, ed. Southern, p. 107; Anselm, *Commendatio*, *SAO*, 2, p. 41.

Commendatio to *De incarnatione*. On the basis of parallels of style and subject matter, Schmitt contended that *Commendatio*'s authorial affiliation is to *Cur Deus homo* instead.[255] While I believe he erred, the question of which one of the two treatises *Commedatio* should preface does not affect the following argument.[256] What matters here is that Anselm gifted a copy of his work, either *De incarnatione* or *Cur Deus homo*, to Pope Urban II.

Commendatio comprises two clauses. The first is an *apologia* for rationalistic theology. The opening states that the Fathers explicated Christian principles from reason in order to contest unbelievers and cultivate believers. Then comes the crux: that endeavour should be resumed. The reasons are as follows. Patristic expositions did not exhaust the rational basis of faith, which is too enormous for man to chart in its entirety. God bestows his gifts on the faithful until the end of the world. The Bible encourages Christians to seek to understand what they believe. Understanding is a midway point between faith and the revelational sight of God, the latter being the ultimate goal of Christian life. Hence Anselm's own inquiries and their publication for the benefit of others, whom he encourages to assess his work. The final clause requests that Pope Urban approve and, if need be, amend 'the work appended'.

Anselm's other writings, too, articulate validations of his theological method, but never in the same overtly apologetic spirit as does the *Commendatio*.[257] Considering how important justifications of free inquiry are to the history of critical thinking, it is surprising how little attention has been paid to the piece.[258] One major aspect remains unremarked: presenting

---

[255] F. S. Schmitt, 'La lettre de saint Anselme au pape Urbain II à l'occasion de la remise de son *Cur Deus homo* (1098)', *Revue des Sciences Religieuses*, 16 (1936), 129–44.

[256] S. Niskanen, 'Anselm's so-called *Commendatio operis ad Vrbanum papam II*: its affiliation, transmission, and a new critical edition', *Revue d'histoire des textes*, 17 (forthcoming, 2022).

[257] Anselm, *Monologion*, Prologus; *Proslogion*, Prooemium; *Cur Deus homo*, i.1–2; *SAO*, 1, pp. 7–8, 93–4, and *SAO*, 2, pp. 47–50 respectively.

[258] The fullest commentary is C. Stercal, 'Educare e maturare la fede nell' intelligenza: "intellectum esse medium intelligo"', in I. Biffi, C. Marabelli and

Commendatio to Urban II was an act of promoting rationalistic discussion about faith to the highest ecclesiastical authority. Such a purpose resonates with my reading of Hugh of Die's injunction to Anselm; the legate implicitly endorsed the method of inquiry applied in the *Monologion* and *Proslogion*. On committing *Commendatio* to Pope Urban, Anselm's position was, of course, very different to the late 1070s when he wrote those two treatises and when, some years later, Hugh ordered him to publish them under his own name. Preferment to the archbishopric of Canterbury in 1093 had elevated Anselm to heights at which criticisms by readers could hardly impinge. Even so, *Commendatio* should be seen as a device to amplify the apostolic endorsement for his theological method, which was first pronounced by Hugh and was subsequently brought to perfection at the Council of Bari.

Commendatio has yet another lesson for us, deriving from its manuscripts. In fifteen of the twenty-two survivors it is prefixed to *Cur Deus homo*, most often as its final paratext after a prologue proper and a list of chapter headings. Significantly, while placing *Commendatio* that way, eight copies of the said sub-group furnish it with the heading 'Prologus Anselmi de incarnatione uerbi', with some textual variation.[259] It is a striking disagreement that *Commendatio* is affiliated to *De incarnatione* by heading and to *Cur Deus homo* by placing. Given that these eight manuscripts position *Commendatio* after the prologue to *Cur Deus homo*, and in most cases also its list of contents, only a most inattentive copyist would not have noticed an incongruence so apparent. We may assume that at least some of them, if not all, were alive to the problem. Some copyists harmonised the discrepancy by

S. M. Malaspina (eds.), *Anselmo d'Aosta educatore europeo: Convegno di studi, Saint-Vincent 7–8 maggio 2002* (Milan: Jaca Books, 2003), pp. 61–82.

[259]   Melk, Benediktinerstift, Cod. 6 (xiii$^{1/2}$, Melk); Zürich, Zentralbibliothek, Rh. 124 (xii, Rheinau); Venice, Biblioteca Nazionale Marciana, Lat. Cl. II 1 (xii$^{2/2}$–xiii$^{1/2}$, Germany); St Gallen, Stiftsbibliothek, Cod. Sang. 801 (before 1428, St Gallen); Vienna, Österreichische Nationalbibliothek, Cod. 691 (xii$^{3/4}$, Göttweig); Kassel, Universitätsbibliothek, Theol. 4° 27 (xii$^{2/2}$, Hardehausen); Oxford, Bodleian Library, Laud misc. 457 (*c.*1200–10, Eberbach); Berlin, Staatsbibliothek, Theol. Lat. Qu. 171 (xv$^{med.}$, Erfurt).

omitting or modifying the heading: variants such as 'Prologus',[260] 'Prefatio libri',[261] 'Excusatio et commendatio operis ad Vrbanum papam',[262] and 'Epistola ad Vrbanum papam'[263] emerged in the process.[264] These approaches to the heading – deliberate negligence, omission and modification – embody reflexion at various stages of transmission as to how to serve *Commendatio* to readers in the face of a perceived misidentification of its mother text. Even if associated also with another treatise in their exemplars, copyists considered the address to Pope Urban an adornment to *Cur Deus homo*. The new headings 'Excusatio et commendatio operis ad Vrbanum papam' and 'Epistola ad Vrbanum papam' demonstrate that the papal aspect carried prestige.

---

[260] BnF, lat. 17456 (xii$^{3/4}$, northern France).

[261] Munich, Universitätsbibliothek, 2° Cod. 105 (xiv, Ingolstadt).

[262] Erfurt, Universitätsbibliothek, CA 2° 83 (1466).

[263] Cologne, Historisches Archiv, W 137 (xii$^{2/2}$, owned at Niederwerth).

[264] A heading with a reference to *Cur Deus homo*: Munich, Bayerische Staatsbibliothek, clm 27319 (1477 × 1484, Andechs); Berlin, Staatsbibliothek, Magdeb. 34 (1452, Germany). No heading: St Gallen, Cod. Sang. 287 (xii$^{1/2}$, St Gallen).

6 Conclusions

The author of an anonymous twelfth-century *accessus* proposed that Arator deployed 'two letters as a prologue, one of which is to Abbot Florianus, so that he would be more eagerly received since a great man reads him'.[265] In other words, the commentator maintained that a dedicatory proem addressed to an important person was the instrument by which an author might attract potential readerships. This was certainly a major incentive for the four writers studied here to report their papal connexions in prefatory texts. An apostolic bond bestowed an aura of authority. Rome could have been engaged in several ways and at various levels of commitment. Fulcoius's presentation of a copy of his biblical epic to Pope Alexander II and Hildebrand did not elicit any effective response. Even so, the affair made them members of Fulcoius' publishing circle, a modern conceptualisation of social conduits by which medieval authors sought and found audiences.[266] Resembling Abbot Florianus' function in the quoted *accessus*, the role of Alexander and Hildebrand proved entirely passive. Genuine endorsement could naturally make a great difference. Arator benefitted from Pope Vigilius' extraordinary contribution towards the publication of the *Historia apostolica*. When he soon afterwards despatched the work to Gaul, he cited the pope's engagement as bait. By his own account, Anselm was prompted by a papal legate to take the decisive step from anonymity to authorial self-assertion. The legate's apostolic command that Anselm sign his treatises was, then, a crucial juncture in one of the great intellectual trajectories of the medieval West. The idealised relationship between Jerome and Pope Damasus – a medieval tradition with vigorous continuations in early-modern painting – demonstrates the potential that papal endorsement could possess in the long run.

Our case-studies suggest that a quid pro quo was a factor for Rome. A momentous undertaking in its own right, Jerome's translation of the

---

[265] *Accessus*, ed. Wheeler, p. 46: 'Et facit duas epistolas quibus utitur pro prologo, unam Floriano abbati, ut tanto acceptabilior sit cum legat eum tantus uir.' Cf. n. 125 above.

[266] See n. 2 above.

Gospels was an adornment for Damasus, an energetic pope who launched large-scale enterprises. Damasus also reformed the liturgy to a profound extent, a project for which the new Gospel translation bore some relevance.[267] A eulogy to the Petrine primacy, Arator's *Historia apostolica* gave wings to Pope Vigilius' claims to that effect. Completed at a time of peril, the work also gave the pope an opportunity to arrange a series of mass meetings in the form of an authorial recital in order to rally support within Rome's clergy, nobility and *populus*. When he received Hugh of Die's legatine endorsement in 1083 × 1085, Anselm was in charge of a vigorous monastic community, the abbey of Bec, renowned for its school and teachers. The papacy regarded the house as an ally in Normandy, as is demonstrated by Pope Gregory VII's letter to Anselm. Furthermore, Hugh, who was an avid reader of patristic literature, must have recognised in Anselm an extraordinary monastic intellectual. Subsequently, in 1098, Pope Urban II needed Anselm's expertise in an upcoming council, where he was duly endorsed in front of the delegates. The concept of reciprocity also helps us appreciate Fulcoius' failure to stimulate enthusiasm in the curia. A secular priest with allegiance to a man who proved the archenemy of papal reformers in France, he did not have much to offer. His biblical versification is an admirable literary achievement, but lent no benefit to reformist policies such as the abolishment of simony and clerical concubinage. Rome had no particular reason to sponsor an author with Fulcoius' credentials.

Two of our authors held office at Rome. This gave them a high level of access to the pope. Arator's office of subdeacon was possibly a sinecure position to provide for his writing. The translation of the Gospels was part of Jerome's assignment as a papal secretary. Figure 1 presented in the Introduction suggests that the extension of papal government from the mid-eleventh century onwards created new opportunities for men of letters. Pamphleteers, for instance, profited by the escalation in Roman activism. One such was Peter Damian, a monk and prior of Monte Avellana, who, as

---

[267] M. H. Shepherd, Jr, 'The liturgical reform of Damasus I', in P. Granfield and J. A. Jungmann (eds.), *Kyriakon. Festschrift Johannes Quasten*, 2 vols. (Münster: Aschendorff, 1970), vol. II, pp. 847–63, at 848.

indicated by the quantitative evidence from the *Patrologia Latina*, was the apparent herald of that new phase. He was made cardinal bishop of Ostia in 1057, and he subsequently held several papal legateships. He authored a large body of writings with considerable success, as is witnessed by the almost 700 extant manuscripts conveying his words.[268] Years before his recruitment to the college of cardinals, he had emerged as a major ideologist of the papal reform movement and could tap into that association in ingenious ways. A case in point is his *Liber Gomorrhianus*, an attack on clerical sodomy, written in 1049. The text opens with a dedicatory letter to Pope Leo IX, whom Peter readdressed at the conclusion in order to solicit a written response to specific questions. Having obtained it, he had it prefixed to the work as a proem.[269] Peter's publishing is a fascinating case also by virtue of relatively ample anecdotal evidence, mainly from his letters and their manuscripts, as to how copies of his works were produced, preserved, edited and distributed under his oversight.[270] In the next century, reformist pamphleteering with repeated resort to publishing circles including papal agents was an option also in transalpine Europe. For instance, various papal parties were involved, one way or another, in the publication of eleven of the twenty known treatises of Gerhoh of Reichersberg (†1169), a German publicist of reformist causes.[271] It has been argued that the investiture contest between church and state over the right to appoint bishops and abbots, a concomitant of the papal reform, was crucial to the formation of 'the public sphere' in Europe.[272] While that application of the

---

[268] K. Reindel, 'Neue Literatur zu Petrus Damiani', *Deutsches Archiv für Erforschung des Mittelalters*, 32 (1976), 405–43, at 406.

[269] Peter Damian, *Ep.* 31, ed. K. Reindel, *Die Briefe des Petrus Damiani*, MGH, *Die Briefe der deutschen Kaiserzeit*, 4, 4 vols. (Munich: MGH, 1983–93), vol. I, pp. 285–7, 329–30.

[270] K. Reindel, 'Studien zur Überlieferung der Werke des Petrus Damiani I', *Deutsches Archiv für Erforschung des Mittelalters*, 15 (1959), 23–102, at 50–67.

[271] P. Classen, *Gerhoch von Reichersberg. Eine Biographie mit einem Anhang über die Quellen, ihre handschriftliche Überlieferung und ihre Chronologie* (Wiesbaden: Steiner, 1960), pp. 407–27.

[272] L. Melve, *Inventing the Public Sphere: The Public Debate During the Investiture Contest (c.1030–1122)* (Leiden: Brill, 2007).

term, coined by Jürgen Habermas to capture early-modern discursive realities, has also met with criticism, causes supported by the reform papacy certainly provoked coherent polemical discourses conducted exceptionally far and wide for a prolonged period.[273] Studies on how polemicists such as Peter Damian and Gerhoh published are a desideratum.

The same applies to those popes who were authors. As noted in the Introduction, the corpus of Pope Gregory I's writings is an anomaly by its size in the history of the (early) medieval papacy. What is more, many of the channels by which he reached distant audiences would have been unavailable in the following centuries as the collapse of imperial administrative apparatuses severed the ties of interregional communication. Gregory's main significance for scholarship on medieval publication would, then, be as a representative of late-Roman authors, who could compose in reasonable hopes that their works would reach distant regions within months or even weeks of their first publication.[274] A comparison with Innocent III (†1216) would be fruitful, with the proviso that the dearth of anecdotal evidence on his publishing rather restricts the view. He, too, obtained extensive contemporary readerships, especially for his *De miseria humanae conditionis*, which he wrote while a cardinal.[275] The conduits of publication at the turn of the sixth and twelfth centuries differed from each other in respect of institutional networks and the professionals involved in the process. As a result, a comparative focus on these two popes could help us observe how the mechanics of communication were transformed in the Middle Ages.

What remained a constant in the procedures of medieval publication was a reliance on the manuscript book. Presentation manuscripts serving a crucial function featured in three of our four case-studies. Arator gave a copy of the *Historia apostolica* to the pope, who in turn instructed his chief

---

[273] C. Symes, review of Melve, *Inventing the Public Sphere*, *American Historical Review*, 114 (2009), 468–9.

[274] For pertinent results from the necessary spadework already undertaken, see L. Castaldi (ed.), *Gregorius I Papa*, *La trasmissione dei testi latini del Medievo*, 5 (Florence: SISMEL, 2013).

[275] See Sharpe, 'Anselm as author', 3–5 with notes to earlier scholarship.

of staff to deposit it in the papal library. Conducted in the presence of an invited clerical audience, the event became a ceremony. Fulcoius gifted a copy of his poem to Pope Alexander II and Hildebrand. Anselm gave Pope Urban II a presentation manuscript with a dedicatory note, the *Commendatio*, purposed exclusively for the occasion. None of these volumes is known to be extant. The survival rate of presentation copies improves towards the end of the era, and their functionality in the papal court continued for generations after the emergence of literary composition in the vernacular and the introduction of the printed book.[276] Presentation copies are physical evidence of how authors advanced their careers and causes, and they will provide fresh insights into the nexus between the papacy and publication.[277]

---

[276] E.g. Naples, Biblioteca Nazionale, I G 40, Jean Mallard's French paraphrase of the Lord's Prayer, and Biblioteca Apostolica Vaticana, Vat. lat. 5536, a Latin translation of Martin de Brion's *Tresample description de toute la Terre Saincte*, gifted by the authors to Cardinal Alessandro Farnese (†1589) and Pope Paul III (†1549) respectively.

[277] Cf. J. P. Carley, '"Deditissimus seruus". Jean Mallard's book presentations to Francis I, Henry VIII and others: their form and function', in G. Müller-Oberhäuser (ed.), *Book Gifts and Cultural Networks from the 14th to the 16th Century* (Münster: Rhema, 2019), pp. 145–63, at 158.

Abbreviations

AD   Archives départementales

BM   Bibliothèque municipale / Médiathèque

BnF   Paris, Bibliothèque nationale de France

CCCM   *Corpus Christianorum. Continuatio Mediaevalis*, 1– (Turnhout: Brepols, 1971–).

CCSL   *Corpus Christianorum. Series Latina*, 1– (Turnhout: Brepols, 1954–).

CLA   *Codices Latini Antiquiores. A Palaeographical Guide to Latin Manuscripts Prior to the Ninth Century*, 11 vols. and Supplement (Oxford: Clarendon Press, 1935–71; 2nd ed. of vol. II, 1972).

CSEL   *Corpus Scriptorum Ecclesiasticorum Latinorum*, 1– (Vienna: Tempsky, 1866–).

Ep(p).   *Epistola(e), Epistula(e)*

ICUR   *Inscriptiones christianae urbis Romae septimo saeculo antiquiores*, ed. G. de Rossi, 2 vols. (Rome: Libraria Pontificia, 1857–88).

lat.   latin

MGH   Monumenta Germaniae Historica

MS   manuscript

PL   *Patrologiae Cursus Completus. Series Latina*, ed. J.-P. Migne, 217 vols. (Paris, 1844–55).

SAO   *Sancti Anselmi Opera Omnia*, ed. F. S. Schmitt, 6 vols. (Seckau, Rome, Edinburgh, 1938–61).

References

Manuscripts Cited

Angers
   BM
      24(20)

Beauvais
   BM
      11

Berlin
   Staatsbibliothek
      Magdeb. 34
      Theol. Lat. Qu. 171

Cambridge
   Trinity College
      B. 14. 3
      B. 16. 44

Châlons-en-Champagne
   AD Marne
      13 H 72 n° 1

Chartres
   BM
      497

Cologne
>   Historisches Archiv
>>   W 137

Erfurt
>   Universitätsbibliothek
>>   CA 2° 83

Kassel
>   Universitätsbibliothek
>>   Theol. 4° 27

Meaux
>   BM
>>   63

Melk
>   Benediktinerstift
>>   Cod. 6

Munich
>   Bayerische Staatsbibliothek
>>   clm 27319
>   Universitätsbibliothek
>>   2° Cod. 105

Naples
>   Biblioteca Nazionale
>>   I G 40

Oxford

  Bodleian Library

    Laud misc. 457

Paris

  Bibliothèque de l'Arsenal

    713

  BnF

    lat. 1
    lat. 2773
    lat. 3854
    lat. 5305
    lat. 5905
    lat. 8095
    lat. 9347
    lat. 16701
    lat. 17456

Reims

  AD Marne

    2 G 2158 n° 1
    56 H 268
    56 H 525
    56 H 980
    57 H 1

St Gallen

  Stiftsbibliothek

    Cod. Sang. 287
    Cod. Sang. 801
    Cod. Sang. 1395

Vatican City

  Biblioteca Apostolica Vaticana

    Pal. lat. 833
    Vat. lat. 5536

Venice
  Biblioteca Nazionale Marciana
    Lat. Cl. II 1

Vienna
  Österreichische Nationalbibliothek
    Cod. 691

Wolfenbüttel
  Herzog-August-Bibliothek
    Weißenburg 76

Zürich
  Zentralbibliothek
    Rh. 124

Printed Primary Sources

Accessus ad Auctores: Medieval Introductions to the Authors (Codex latinus monacensis 19475), ed. and tr. S. M. Wheeler (Kalamazoo: Medieval Institute Publications, 2015).

Alexander of Canterbury, *Liber de dictis beati Anselmi*, in *Memorials of St Anselm*, ed. R. W. Southern and F. S. Schmitt (Oxford University Press, 1969), pp. 105–270.

Anselm, *Cur Deus homo*, *SAO*, 2, pp. 37–133.

  Commendatio operis ad Vrbanum papam II, *SAO*, 2, pp. 39–41.

  Epistola de incarnatione Verbi, *SAO*, 2, pp. 1–35.

  Epistolae, ed. S. Niskanen, *Letters of Anselm, Archbishop of Canterbury, I: The Bec Letters* (Oxford University Press, 2019), and for his Canterbury letters, *SAO*, 3–5. The former cited by letter and section numbers.

Monologion, *SAO*, 1, pp. 1–87.

Proslogion, *SAO*, 1, pp. 89–139.

Arator, *Historia apostolica*, ed. B. Bureau and P.-A. Deproost, *Arator: Histoire apostolique* (Paris: Les Belles Lettres, 2017); English tr. with introduction and notes, R. Hillier (Liverpool University Press, 2020). Cited by section and line numbers.

Arnulf of Lisieux, *Invectiva in Girardum*, ed. J. Dieterich, MGH, *Libelli de lite*, 3 (Hanover: Hahn, 1897), pp. 85–107.

Augustine, *Epistulae*, ed. A Goldbacher, *CSEL*, 34/2 (1898). Cited by letter and section numbers.

Bernold of Constance, *De reordinatione vitanda et de salute parvulorum qui ab excommunicatis baptiẓati sunt*, ed. F. Thaner, MGH, *Libelli de lite*, 2 (Hanover: Hahn, 1892), pp. 150–56.

Eadmer, *Historia nouorum in Anglia*, ed. M. Rule, Rolls Series (London: Longman, 1884).

Vita S. Anselmi, ed. R. W. Southern (Oxford University Press, 1972).

Decretales pseudo-Isidorianae et capitula Angilramni, ed. P. Hinschius (Leipzig: Tauchnitz, 1863).

Decretum Gelasianum de libris recipiendis et non recipiendis, ed. E. von Dobschütz (Leipzig: Hinrichs, 1912).

Fulcoius of Beauvais, *Epistulae*, ed. M. L. Colker, in *Traditio*, 10 (1954), 191–273.

Vtriusque de nuptiis Christi et ecclesiae libri septem, ed. M. I. J. Rousseau (Washington, DC: The Catholic University of America Press, 1960). Cited by section and line numbers.

Geoffroy of Tiron, *Vita beati Bernardi*, *PL*, 172, cols. 1363–1446.

Gregory I, *Registrum epistularum*, ed. P. Ewald and R. Hartmann, MGH, *Epistolae*, 1–2 (Berlin: Weidmann, 1891–9).

Gregory VII, *Registrum*, ed. E. Caspar, MGH, *Epistolae selectae*, 2, 2nd ed., 2 vols. (Berlin: Weidmann, 1955).

Gregory Nazianzen, *Carmina moralia*, *Patrologia Graeca*, 37 (Paris: Apud J.-P. Migne, 1862), cols. 397–1600.

Gregory of Tours, *Libri historiarum X*, ed. B. Krusch and W. Levison, MGH, *Scriptores rerum Merovingicarum*, 1 (Hanover: Hahn, 1951).

'Hieronymus noster', *PL*, 22, cols. 175–84.

Hugh of Amiens, *Contra haereticos sui temporis sive de ecclesia et eius ministris libri tres*, *PL*, 192, cols. 1255–98.

Inscriptiones Christianae urbis Romae septimo saeculo antiquiores, ed. G. de Rossi, 2 vols. (Rome: Libraria Pontificia, 1857–88).

Ivo of Chartres, *Collectio tripartita*, https://ivo-of-chartres.github.io/tripartita.html, accessed 5 May 2021.

   Decretum, https://ivo-of-chartres.github.io/decretum.html, accessed 5 May 2021.

Jerome, *Apologia aduersus libros Rufini*, ed. P. Lardet, *CCSL*, 79 (1982), pp. 1–72.

   Commentariorum in Esaiam libri I–XI, ed. M. Adriaen, *CCSL*, 73, 2 vols. (1963).

   De uiris illustribus, ed. E. Richardson, *Texte und Untersuchungen zur Geschichte der altchristlichen Literatur*, 14, 1a (Leipzig: Hinrichs, 1896), pp. 1–56. Cited by section number.

   Epistulae, ed. I. Hilberg, *CSEL*, 54–6 (1910–18) and ed. J. Divjak, *CSEL*, 88 (1981). Cited by letter and section numbers; the latter indicated by asterisk.

   Praefatio ad Paulinianum in libro Didymi Alexandrini de Spiritu sancto, *PL*, 23, cols. 101–4.

   Praefatio in Evangelio, *Biblia Sacra iuxta Vulgatam versionem*, ed. R. Weber, 3rd ed. (Stuttgart: Deutsche Bibelgesellschaft, 1983), pp. 1515–16.

   Praefatio in Origenis homiliis II in Canticum, ed. W. A. Baehrens, *Corpus Berolinense*, 33 (Berlin: Brandenburgische Akademie der Wissenschaften, 1925), p. 26.

John Beleth, *Summa de ecclesiasticis officiis*, ed. H. Douteil, *CCCM*, 41, 2 vols. (1976).

John of Echternach, *De tribus missis in nativitate Domini celebrandis*, *PL*, 166, cols. 1509–14.

Juvencus, *Euangeliorum libri IV*, ed. J. Huemer, *CSEL*, 24 (1891).

Lawrence of Durham, *Hypognosticon*, Prologus, in *Dialogi Laurentii Dunelmensis monachi ac prioris*, ed. J. Raine, Surtees Society, 70 (1880).

Liber diurnus Romanorum pontificum ou Recueil des formules usitées par la chancellerie pontificale du Ve au XIe siècle, ed. E. Rozière (Paris: Durand et Pedone-Lauriel, 1869).

Liber pontificalis, ed. L. Duchesne, *Le Liber pontificalis: texte, introduction et commentaire*, 2 vols. (Paris: Thorin, 1886–92).

Nicholas I, *Epistolae*, ed. E. Perels, MGH, *Epistolae*, 6 (Berlin: Weidmann, 1925), pp. 257–690.

Nicola Maniacutia, *Vita S. Hieronymi*, *PL*, 22, cols. 183–202.

Obituarium Lugdunensis ecclesiae: Nécrologe des personnages illustres et des bienfaiteurs de l'église métropolitaine de Lyon du IXe au XVe siècle, ed. M.-C. Guigue (Lyon: Scheuring, 1867).

Osbert of Clare, *Epistolae*, ed. E. W. Williamson, *Letters of Osbert of Clare, Prior of Westminster* (Oxford University Press, 1929).

Peter Damian, *Epistolae*, ed. K. Reindel, *Die Briefe des Petrus Damiani*, MGH, *Die Briefe der deutschen Kaiserzeit*, 4, 4 vols. (Munich: MGH, 1983–93).

Peter of Poitiers, *Epistola ad Petrum abbatem Cluniacensem*, *PL*, 189, col. 47.

Procopius, *History of the Wars*, tr. H. Dewing, Loeb Classical Library, 5 vols. (Cambridge, MA: Harvard University Press, 1914–28).

Recueil des actes de Philippe Ier, ed. M. Prou (Paris: Imprimerie Nationale, 1908).

Rufinus, *De adulteratione librorum Origenis*, ed. M. Simonetti, *CCSL*, 20 (1961).

Sedulius, *Carmen paschale*, ed. J. Huemer, *CSEL*, 10 (1885).

Urban II, *Epistolae*, *PL*, 151, cols. 283–552.

Venantius Fortunatus, *Vita sancti Martini*, ed. S. Quesnel, *Venace Fortunat: Vie de Saint Martin* (Paris: Les Belles Lettres, 1996).

Secondary Sources

Baldovin, J. F., *The Urban Character of Christian Worship. The Origins, Development, and Meaning of Stational Liturgy* (Rome: Pont. Institutum Studiorum Orientalium, 1987).

Bignami-Odier, J., 'Une lettre apocryphe de saint Damase à saint Jérôme sur la question de Melchisédech', *Mélanges d'archéologie et d'histoire*, 63 (1951), 183–90.

Blanchard, P., 'La correspondance apocryphe du pape S. Damase et de S. Jérôme sur le psautier et le chant de l'alleluia', *Ephemerides Liturgicae*, 63 (1949), 376–88.

Bloch, R. H., *God's Plagiarist: Being an Account of the Fabulous Industry and Irregular Commerce of the Abbé Migne* (University of Chicago Press, 1994).

Bogaert, P.-M., 'The Latin Bible', in J. Carleton Paget and J. Schaper (eds.), *The New Cambridge History of the Bible, I. From the Beginnings to 600* (Cambridge University Press, 2013), pp. 505–26.

Boutémy, A., 'Essai de chronologie des poésies de Foulcoie de Beauvais', *Annuaire de l'Institut de philologie et d'histoire orientales et slaves*, 11 (1951), 79–96.

Bureau, B., 'Parthenius et la question de l'authenticité de la Lettre à Parthenius d'Arator', in B. Bureau and C. Nicolas (eds.), *Moussyllanea. Mélanges de linguistique et de littérature anciennes offerts à Claude Moussy* (Leuven: Peeters, 1998), pp. 387–97.

Cain, A., 'In Ambrosiaster's shadow: a critical re-evaluation of the last surviving letter exchange between Pope Damasus and Jerome', *Revue d'études augustiniennes et patristiques*, 51 (2005), 257–77.

'The letter collections of Jerome of Stridon', in Sogno et al. (eds.), *Late Antique Letter Collections* (Oakland: University of California Press, 2017), pp. 221–38.

The Letters of Jerome: Asceticism, Biblical Exegesis, and the Construction of Christian Authority in Late Antiquity (Oxford University Press, 2009).

Cameron, A., *The Last Pagans of Rome* (Oxford University Press, 2011).

Carley, J. P., '"Deditissimus seruus". Jean Mallard's book presentations to Francis I, Henry VIII and others: their form and function', in G. Müller-Oberhäuser (ed.), *Book Gifts and Cultural Networks from the 14th to the 16th Century* (Münster: Rhema, 2019), pp. 145–63.

Castaldi, L. (ed.), *Gregorius I Papa, La trasmissione dei testi latini del Medievo*, 5 (Florence: SISMEL, 2013).

Classen, P., *Gerhoch von Reichersberg. Eine Biographie mit einem Anhang über die Quellen, ihre handschriftliche Überlieferung und ihre Chronologie* (Wiesbaden: Steiner, 1960).

Colker, M. L., 'Fulcoius of Beauvais, poet and propagandist', in Herren et al. (eds.), *Latin Culture in the Eleventh Century*, vol. I (Turnhout: Brepols, 2002), pp. 144–57.

Cowdrey, H. E. J., *Gregory VII 1073–1085* (Oxford: Clarendon Press, 1998).

Lanfranc: Scholar, Monk, and Archbishop (Oxford University Press, 2003).

'The Papacy and the Berengarian Controversy', in P. Ganz, R. Huygens and F. Niewöhner (eds.), *Auctoritas und Ratio: Studien zu Berengar von Tours* (Wiesbaden: Otto Harrassowitz, 1990), pp. 109–38.

De Bruyn, T. S., Cooper, S. A. and Hunter, D. G., *Ambrosiaster's Commentary on the Pauline Epistles: Romans* (Atlanta: SBL Press, 2017).

De Bruyne, D., 'Gaudiosus, un vieux libraire romain', *Revue Bénédictine*, 30 (1913), 343–5.

Dinkova-Bruun, G., 'Biblical versifications from late antiquity to the middle of the thirteenth century: history or allegory?', in W. Otten and

K. Pollman (eds.), *Poetry and Exegesis in Premodern Latin Christianity. The Encounter between Classical and Christian Strategies of Interpretation* (Leiden: Brill, 2007), pp. 315–42.

Dupont, F., '*Recitatio* and the reorganization of the space of public discourse', in T. Habinek and A. Schiesaro (eds.), *The Roman Cultural Revolution* (Cambridge University Press, 1997), pp. 44–59.

Dutton, P. E. and Kessler, H. L., *The Poetry and Paintings of the First Bible of Charles the Bald* (Ann Arbor: The University of Michigan Press, 1997).

Duval, Y.-M., 'Sur trois lettres méconnues de Jérôme concernant son séjour à Rome (382–385)', in A. Cain and J. Lössl (eds.), *Jerome of Stridon: His Life, Writings and Legacy* (Farnham: Ashgate, 2007), pp. 29–40.

Fontaine, J., 'Education and learning', in P. Fouracre (ed.), *The New Cambridge Medieval History, I: c. 500–c.700* (Cambridge University Press, 2005), pp. 735–59.

Franklin, A., *Les anciennes bibliothèques de Paris*, 3 vols. (Paris: Imprimerie Impériale, 1867–74).

Franklin, C. V., 'The epigraphic *syllogae* of BAV, Palatinus Latinus 833', in J. Hamesse (ed.), *Roma, magistra mundi. Itineraria culturae medievalis. Mélanges offert au Père L. E. Boyle à l'occasion de son 75e anniversaire*, 3 vols. (Louvain-la-Neuve: FIDEM, 1998), vol. II, pp. 975–90.

Freeburn, R. B., *Hugh of Amiens and the Twelfth-Century Renaissaince* (Farnham: Ashgate, 2011).

Gaehde, J. E., 'The Bible of San Paolo fuori le mura in Rome and its date and its relation to Charles the Bald', *Gesta*, 5 (1966), 9–21.

Gameson, R., 'The material fabric of early British books', in R. Gameson (ed.), *The Cambridge History of the Book in Britain*, vol. 1 (Cambridge University Press, 2012), pp. 11–93.

Gasper, G. E. M., 'Envy, jealousy, and the boundaries of orthodoxy: Anselm of Canterbury and the genesis of the *Proslogion*', *Viator*, 41 (2010), 45–68.

Green, R. P. H., *Latin Epics of the New Testament: Juvencus, Sedulius, Arator* (Oxford University Press, 2006).

Haye, T., 'Christliche und pagane Dichtung bei Fulcoius von Beauvais', in M. W. Herren, C. J. McDonough and R. G. Arthur (eds.), *Latin Culture in the Eleventh Century*, vol. I (Turnhout: Brepols, 2002), pp. 398–409.

  Päpste und Poeten. Die mittelalterliche Kurie als Objekt und Förderer panegyrischer Dichtung (Berlin: De Gruyter, 2009).

Heikkinen, S., 'The Christianization of Latin metre: a study of Bede's *De arte metrica*', unpublished PhD thesis, University of Helsinki (2012).

Herren, M. W., McDonough, C. J. and Arthur, R. G. (eds.), *Latin Culture in the Eleventh Century: Proceedings of the Third International Conference on Medieval Latin Studies (Cambridge, 9–12 September 1998)*, 2 vols. (Turnhout: Brepols, 2002).

Hillier, R., *Arator on the Acts of the Apostoles: A Baptismal Commentary* (Oxford: Clarendon Press, 1993).

Hobbins, D., *Authorship and Publicity before Print: Jean Gerson and the Transformation of Late Medieval Learning* (Philadelphia: University of Pennsylvania Press, 2009).

Houghton, H. A. G., *The Latin New Testament: A Guide to Early History, Texts and Manuscripts* (Oxford University Press, 2016).

Jahn, O., 'Über die Subscriptionen in den Handschriften römischer Classiker', *Berichte über die Verhandlungen der Königlich-Sächsischen Gesellschaft der Wissenschaften zu Leipzig, Philologisch-Historische Klasse*, 3 (Leipzig: Weidmannsche Buchhandlung, 1851), pp. 327–72.

Kelly, J. N. D., *Jerome. His Life, Writings, and Controversies* (New York: Harper & Row, 1975).

Knibbs, E., 'Ebo of Reims, Pseudo-Isidore, and the Date of the False Decretals', *Speculum*, 92 (2017), 144–83.

Lansford, T., *The Latin Inscriptions of Rome: A Walking Guide* (Baltimore, MD: The Johns Hopkins University Press, 2009).

Licht, T., '*Aratoris fortuna*: Zu Aufgang und Überlieferung der *Historia apostolica*', in A. Jördens, H. Gärtner, H. Görgemanns and A. Ritter, *Quaerite faciem eius semper. Studien zu den geistesgeschichtlichen Beziehungen zwischen Antike und Christentum. Dankesgabe für Albrecht Dihle aus dem Heidelberger Kirchenväterkolloquium* (Hamburg: Kovac, 2008), pp. 163–79.

Love, H., *Scribal Publication in Seventeenth-Century England* (Oxford: Clarendon Press, 1993).

Lunn-Rockcliffe, S., *Ambrosiaster's Political Theology* (Oxford University Press, 2007).

Manitius, M., *Geschichte der lateinischen Literatur des Mittelalters*, 3 vols. (Munich: Beck, 1911–31).

Marrou, H. I., Review of *Aratoris subdiaconi De actibus apostolorum*, ed. A. P. McKinlay, *Gnomon*, 25 (1954), 253–5.

McGuckin, J., *St. Gregory of Nazianzus: An Intellectual Biography* (New York: St Vladimir's Seminary Press, 2001).

McGurk, P., 'The oldest manuscripts of the Latin Bible', in R. Gameson (ed.), *The Early Medieval Bible: Its Production, Decoration and Use* (Cambridge University Press, 1994), pp. 1–23.

McKitterick, R., *Rome and the Invention of the Papacy: The* Liber Pontificalis (Cambridge University Press, 2020).

Melve, L., *Inventing the Public Sphere: The Public Debate During the Investiture Contest (*c.*1030–1122)* (Leiden: Brill, 2007).

Mews, C. J., 'St Anselm, Roscelin and the See of Beauvais', in D. E. Luscombe and G. R. Evans (eds.), *Anselm: Aosta, Bec and Canterbury: Papers in Commemoration of the Nine-Hundredth Anniversary of Anselm's Enthronement as Archbishop, 25 September 1093* (Sheffield Academic Press, 1996), pp. 106–19.

'St Anselm and Roscelin: some new texts and their implications. I. The *De incarnatione Verbi* and the *Disputatio inter christianum et gentilem*', *Archives d'histoire doctrinale et littéraire du Moyen Âge*, 58 (1991), 55–98.

Moser, T. C., Jr, *A Cosmos of Desire. The Medieval Latin Erotic Lyric in English Manuscripts* (Ann Arbor: The University of Michigan Press, 2004).

Nautin, P., 'Le premier échange épistolaire entre Jérôme et Damase: lettres réelles ou fictives?', *Freiburger Zeitschrift für Philosophie und Theologie*, 30 (1983), 331–44.

Niskanen, S., 'Anselm's predicament: the *Proslogion* and anti-intellectual rhetoric in the aftermath of the Berengarian Controversy', *Journal of the History of Ideas*, 82 (2021), 547–68.

'Anselm's so-called *Commendatio operis ad Vrbanum papam II*: its affiliation, transmission, and a new critical edition', *Revue d'histoire des textes*, 17 (forthcoming, 2022).

'Copyists and redactors: Towards a prolegomenon to the *editio princeps* of *Peregrinatio Antiochie per Vrbanum papam facta*', in O. Merisalo, M. Kuha and S. Niiranen (eds.), *Transmission of Knowledge in the Late Middle Ages and the Renaissance* (Turnhout: Brepols, 2019), pp. 103–14.

'The emergence of an authorial culture: publishing in Denmark in the long twelfth century', in A. C. Horn and K. G. Johansson (eds.), *The Meaning of Media. Texts and Materiality in Medieval Scandinavia* (Berlin: De Gruyter, 2021), pp. 71–91.

'From author to authority: Anselm's public reputation and the Council of Bari (1098)', *Journal of Medieval History* (forthcoming).

Omont, H., 'Épitaphes métriques en l'honneur de différents personnages du XIe siècle composées par Foulcoie de Beauvais, archidiacre de Meaux', *Mélanges Julien Havet* (Paris: E. Leroux, 1895), pp. 211–36.

'Recherches sur la bibliothèque de l'église cathédrale de Beauvais', *Memoires de l'institut national de France*, 40 (1916), 1–93.

Omont, H., Molinier, A., Couderc, C. and Coyecque, E., *Catalogue général des manuscrits des bibliothèques publiques de France. Départements. Tome XI: Chartres* (Paris: Plon, 1890).

Ott, J. S., '"Rome and Reims are equals": Archbishop Manasses I (*c.* 1069–80), Pope Gregory VII, and the fortunes of historical exceptionalism', in S. Danielson and E. A. Gatti (eds.), *Envisioning the Bishop: Images and the Episcopacy in the Middle Ages* (Turnhout: Brepols, 2014), pp. 275–302.

Paravicini Bagliani, A., 'Le dediche alla corte dei papi nel duecento e l'autocoscienza intellettuale', *Filologia mediolatina*, 17 (2010), 69–84.

Reindel, K., 'Neue Literatur zu Petrus Damiani', *Deutsches Archiv für Erforschung des Mittelalters*, 32 (1976), 405–43.

'Studien zur Überlieferung der Werke des Petrus Damiani I', *Deutsches Archiv für Erforschung des Mittelalters*, 15 (1959), 23–102.

Rennie, K. R., *Law and Practice in the Age of Reform. The Legatine Work of Hugh of Die (1073–1106)* (Turnhout: Brepols, 2010).

Reutter, U., *Damasus, Bischof von Rom (366–384)* (Tübingen: Mohr Siebeck, 2009).

Rice, E. F., *Saint Jerome in the Renaissance* (Baltimore, ML: The Johns Hopkins University Press, 1985).

Riché, P., *Éducation et culture dans l'occident barbare, VIe–VIIIe siècles* (Paris: Seuil, 1962).

Robinson, I. S., *Henry IV of Germany 1056–1106* (Cambridge University Press, 1999).

Rolker, C., *Canon Law and the Letters of Ivo of Chartres* (Cambridge University Press, 2010).

Rouse, R. H., 'The early library of the Sorbonne II', *Scriptorium*, 21 (1967), 227–51.

Schmitt, F. S., 'La lettre de saint Anselme au pape Urbain II à l'occasion de la remise de son *Cur Deus homo* (1098)', *Revue des Sciences Religieuses*, 16 (1936), 129–44.

Schwietering, J., *Die Demutsformel mittelhochdeutscher Dichter* (Berlin: Weidmann, 1921).

Schwind, J., *Arator-Studien* (Göttingen: Vandenhoeck & Ruprecht, 1990).

Sharpe, R., 'Anselm as author: publishing in the late eleventh century', *Journal of Medieval Latin*, 19 (2009), 1–87.

   A Handlist of the Latin Writers of Great Britain and Ireland before 1540 (Turnhout: Brepols, 1997; supplement with additions and corrections, 2001).

Shepherd, M. H., Jr, 'The liturgical reform of Damasus I', in P. Granfield and J. A. Jungmann (eds.), *Kyriakon. Festschrift Johannes Quasten*, 2 vols. (Münster: Aschendorff, 1970), vol. II, pp. 847–63.

Sogno, C., Storin, B. K. and Watts, E. J. (eds.), *Late Antique Letter Collections: A Critical Introduction and Reference Guide* (Oakland: University of California Press, 2017).

Somerville, R., 'Pope Nicholas I and John Scottus Eriugena: JE 2833', *Zeitschrift der Savigny-Stiftung für Rechtsgeschichte: Kanonistische Abteilung*, 83 (1997), 67–85.

   Pope Urban II's Council of Piacenza (Oxford University Press, 2011).

Sotinel, C., 'Arator, un poète au service de la politique de Pape Vigile?', *Mélanges de l'École française de Rome*, 101 (1989), 805–20.

Southern, R. W., *St Anselm. A Portrait in a Landscape* (Cambridge University Press, 1990).

Stercal, C., 'Educare e maturare la fede nell'intelligenza: "intellectum esse medium intelligo"', in I. Biffi, C. Marabelli and S. M. Malaspina (eds.), *Anselmo d'Aosta educatore europeo: Convegno di studi, Saint-Vincent 7–8 maggio 2002* (Milan: Jaca Books, 2003), pp. 61–82.

Storin, B. K., *Self-Portrait in Three Colors: Gregory of Nazianzus's Epistolary Autobiography* (Oakland: University of California Press, 2019).

Supino Martini, P., 'Aspetti della cultura grafica a Roma fra Gregorio Magno e Gregorio VII', in *Roma nell'alto medievo*, 2 vols. (Spoleto: CISAM, 2001), vol. II, pp. 911–68.

Symes, C., Review of Melve, *Inventing the Public Sphere*, *American Historical Review*, 114 (2009), 468–9.

Tahkokallio, J., *The Anglo-Norman Historical Canon: Publishing and Manuscript Culture* (Cambridge University Press, 2019).
   'The classicization of the Latin curriculum and "the Renaissance of the Twelfth Century": a quantitative study of the codicological evidence', *Viator*, 46 (2015), 129–54.

Tether, L., *Publishing the Grail in Medieval and Renaissance France* (Woodbridge: Boydell and Brewer, 2017).
   'Revisiting the manuscripts of Perceval and the continuations: Publishing practices and authorial transition', *Journal of the International Arthurian Society*, 2 (2015), 20–45.

Thompson, K., *The Monks of Tiron: A Monastic Community and Religious Reform in the Twelfth Century* (Cambridge University Press, 2014).

Trout, D., *Damasus of Rome: The Epigraphic Poetry* (Oxford University Press, 2015).

Usacheva, A., *Knowledge, Language and Intellection from Origen to Gregory Nazianzen. A Selective Survey* (Frankfurt am Main: Peter Lang, 2017).

Van Houts, E., *Married Life in the Middle Ages, 900–1300* (Oxford University Press, 2019).

Verardi, A., *La memoria legittimante: Il* Liber pontificalis *e la chiesa di Roma del secolo VI* (Rome: ISIME, 2016).

Werner, T., *Den Irrtum liquidieren: Bücherverbrennungen im Mittelalter* (Göttingen: Vandenhoeck & Ruprecht, 2007).

References

Wiest, D. H., *The Precensorship of Books (Canons 1384–1386, 1392–1394, 2318,§2). A History and a Commentary* (Washington, DC: The Catholic University of America Press, 1953).

Williams, J. R., 'Manasses I of Rheims and Pope Gregory VII', *American Historical Review*, 54 (1949), 804–24.

Wilmart, A., 'Deux lettres concernant Raoul le Verd, l'ami de saint Bruno', *Revue Bénédictine*, 51 (1939), 257–74.

Wilmart, M., 'Foulcoie de Beauvais, itinéraire d'un intellectuel du XIe siècle', *Bulletin de la Société Littéraire et Historique de la Brie*, 57 (2002), 35–53.

Acknowledgement

I am indebted to Dr James Willoughby, Dr Ben Pohl, Dr Ville Vuolanto, the participants of the Medieval Publication Seminar at the University of Helsinki, the anonymous peer reviewers, and the editors of this series. Any remaining errors of fact or judgement are my own. This project has received funding from the European Union's Horizon 2020 research and innovation programme under grant agreement No. 716538 (MedPub, Medieval Publishing from *c.*1000 to 1500) and from the Academy of Finland under the grant agreement No. 324246 (Authorial Publication in Early Medieval Europe, *c.*400–1000).

Cambridge Elements $\overline{\overline{}}$

Publishing and Book Culture

SERIES EDITOR

Samantha Rayner
University College London

Samantha Rayner is Professor of Publishing and Book Cultures at UCL. She is also Director of UCL's Centre for Publishing, co-Director of the Bloomsbury CHAPTER (Communication History, Authorship, Publishing, Textual Editing and Reading) and co-Chair of the Bookselling Research Network.

ASSOCIATE EDITOR

Leah Tether
University of Bristol

Leah Tether is Professor of Medieval Literature and Publishing at the University of Bristol. With an academic background in medieval French and English literature and a professional background in trade publishing, Leah has combined her expertise and developed an international research profile in book and publishing history from manuscript to digital.

ABOUT THE SERIES

This series aims to fill the demand for easily accessible, quality texts available for teaching and research in the diverse and dynamic fields of Publishing and Book Culture. Rigorously researched and peer-reviewed Elements will be published under themes, or 'Gatherings'. These Elements should be the first check point for researchers or students working on that area of publishing and book trade history and practice: we hope that, situated so logically at Cambridge University Press, where academic publishing in the UK began, it will develop to create an unrivalled space where these histories and practices can be investigated and preserved.

Cambridge Elements ☰

Publishing and Book Culture
Publishing and Book History

Gathering Editor: Andrew Nash
Andrew Nash is Reader in Book History and Director of the
London Rare Books School at the Institute of English Studies,
University of London. He has written books on Scottish and
Victorian Literature, and edited or co-edited numerous
volumes including, most recently, *The Cambridge History of the
Book in Britain, Volume 7* (CUP, 2019).

Gathering Editor: Leah Tether
Leah Tether is Professor of Medieval Literature and Publishing
at the University of Bristol. With an academic background in
medieval French and English literature and a professional
background in trade publishing, Leah has combined her
expertise and developed an international research profile in
book and publishing history from manuscript to digital.

Elements in the Gathering

Publication and the Papacy in Late Antique and Medieval Europe
Samu Niskanen

A full series listing is available at: www.cambridge.org/EPBC